What Were You Thinking?

Learn How to Change the Way You Think... Fast!

Monica Cornetti

Diane – Think Fast! Monica

Diane - first fast.
Marion

What Were You Thinking?

Learn How to Change the Way You Think... Fast!

Monica Cornetti

Circumference Press

What Were You Thinking? Learn How to Change the Way You Think... Fast!

Copyright © 2014 by Monica Cornetti
Published by Circumference Publishing

All rights reserved. This book may not be used or reproduced in any manner, in whole or in part, stored in a retrieval system or transmitted in any form (by electronic, mechanical, photocopied, recorded or other means) without written permission from the author, except as permitted by United States copyright law.

No liability is assumed with respect to the use of information contained herein. While every precaution has been taken in the preparation of this book, the author assumes no responsibility for errors or omissions. Neither is any liability assumed for damages resulting from the use of information contained herein.

Cover art by Dane Miller at Azure Marketing
Layout by Jonathan Peters, PhD at Circumference Publishing

ISBN: 978-0-9789229-8-6

Printed in the United States of America

Acknowledgments

Many thanks to my family. My parents, who taught me the importance of preparation, practice, and tenacity. My incredibly brave sister Melanie, who I admire more than she will ever know. My older brother Lou, who consistently showed up. And my younger brother Leonard, who nightly challenged me at the kitchen table.

Thanks to my girlfriends Kim, Elyse, Julie, and Gay. My life is enriched and blessed to have you as my BFFs.

A special thanks to my editor and my love Jonathan. My smartest friend, my challenger, my weapon of mass destruction. Thank you for making the *Sandals* commercial a reality.

And finally, an overflow of thankfulness to my creative, talented, curious, and determined sons. Although we don't always agree, and I am often tempted to ask, "What were you thinking?" Lou, Nick, and Joe, I love you too much!

Table of Contents

Prologue	1
Chapter 1: Think BIG!	7
Chapter 2: The Chubby Girl Factor	15
Chapter 3: Ask the Right Questions	25
Chapter 4: Drop the F Bomb	37
Chapter 5: DNF is Not an Option	51
Chapter 6: FUNK in Your TRUNK	61
Chapter 7: Where is Your North?	69
Chapter 8: Out of This World Thinking	81
Chapter 9: Where the Ideas Are	91
Chapter 10: There, Now, How	105
Prologue	115
About the Author	119

The Plays

Drill Down to the Future	12
The Baggage Sweep	20
Right Questions Run	30
RAIN	42
Drop the F Bomb	45
DNF Not an Option	58
FUNK in Your TRUNK	62
Fight the FUNK	66
Where is Your North?	71
Life Line	77
Alien encounter	83
Reverse Assumptions	88
Where the Ideas Are	96
There, Now, How	110

Prologue

As an undergraduate psychology major, my life was changed forever my junior year when I started studying the myriad of theories about human behavior. I didn't realize how complex the human mind could be, and all that went into our behaviors and the way we think.

It was at that time that I knew I would dedicate my life's work and studies to what makes people think the way that they think, make the choices they make, and ultimately why they do the things that they do. At that young age, this new fascination was of course directed towards boys, friends, families, and personal relationships... but over the years, the fascination extended towards the workplace. I began to ask:

- *How do you motivate employees to do what you need them to do?*
- *How can you lead people effectively to reach your business objectives?*
- *How do you encourage creativity, innovation, and lead people to think differently?*

My junior year of college was filled with tons of research and experiments with animals. Test animals had to be closely monitored, so that meant evening and weekend trips to the lab to record food and weight.

One Saturday, still hung over from the previous night's kegger with the boys from St. Vincent's, my best friend Kim and I walked bleary eyed to the lab to check on our animals.

We entered the room where the rats were stored in cages. We started to don gloves and glasses to protect us from the super sharp teeth which the rats were only too willing to sink into whatever flesh they came in contact with. Suddenly we looked at each other. We each had an eerie feeling—you know, the one where you know you are being watched.

Looking around, we realized that the fifty or so rats were not in their cages. They were loose. And all of them were staring at us with their beady rat eyes, just inches from our face and fingers.

I stated the obvious in a surprisingly calm voice, "Kim. There are rats in here. And they are not in their cages."

"Oh my God!" we screamed as the realization hit us. We dropped all of our supplies and ran from the room screaming like a bunch of girls. Slamming the door behind us, we continued jumping around, screaming, and crying in the hall until the security guard came to see what all the commotion was about.

Somehow we managed to get accused of letting the rats out of their cages, and had to convince our Psychology Department Chair that we were not trying to sabotage other students' experiments and ruin their grades.

That particularly unpleasant incident is forever burned in my brain, and still gives me the heebie-jeebies. And yet, it did not deter me from wanting to study more, to read other people's research and to continue the experiments. I was hooked on the study of behaviors and why people do what they do, over and over again, even when they are not getting the results they want or need.

My junior year was also when I learned **The Story of 5 Monkeys**. Although it has been a long time since I originally read the research, I find that it is timeless—and I think you'll agree that you see these same behaviors in your workplace and maybe even in your personal life.

A word of caution as you proceed:
This story may be disturbing to some readers.

Five monkeys were put into a room. In the center of the room was a ladder, and at the top of the ladder a banana hung from the ceiling.
One of the monkeys saw the banana and started to climb the ladder. As he did, all of the monkeys were showered with icy cold water. Each time a monkey would start climbing the ladder, they all would get showered down with icy cold water.
After awhile the monkeys quit trying to go for the banana.
The researcher then took out one of the original monkeys and brought in a new monkey. This little guy sees that banana,

starts to climb the ladder, and as he does, the rest of the monkeys run up to him and beat him up and keep him from going for that banana.

It isn't long before he realizes these other monkeys are not going to let him get that banana, so he stops trying.

A second of the original monkeys is taken out and a new monkey is brought in. He sees the ladder, sees the banana, and starts to go for it. The rest of the monkeys beat him up and keep him from getting there... including that monkey that was never showered with icy cold water.

The researchers did this again and again, replacing original monkeys with new monkeys.

Finally, the cage had five monkeys of whom none had experienced the icy water treatment. The researchers then introduced a new monkey to the cage. When this monkey tried to reach for the banana, all five monkeys ran up to him and beat him up to keep him from getting that banana.

> *You've heard the saying, "Monkey see. Monkey do?" Turns out it's true.*

It's important to realize that none of the monkeys knew why they were beating up this new guy and preventing him from getting the banana; they just knew that's how it's done around here.

None of these monkeys knew about the punishment of icy water, none of them knew why they were not allowed to get the banana, but somewhere along the way they learned that reaching for the banana was not allowed. They became the guardians of this rule without knowing its purpose.

All organizations develop routines, habits, and practices. Very often, nobody actually remembers why the procedures were started in the first place. It's simply a matter of:

"That's the way we've always done it!"

Once we think we know how something should be done, we keep doing it. Then we teach others to do it the same way. And they, in turn, teach others. Until eventually you reach a point where no one remembers why something is done a certain way. But we keep doing it anyway.

Orderly, predictable thoughts lead to methodical, habitual behaviors. Habits are useful, even necessary, but they can turn out routine thinking, which produces the same old results. If we're happy with the results we're getting, then we should continue with the habit.

But if we need to be creative, if we need a different result, then we need to break away from conventional thinking and look for ways to disrupt the habits.

And that is what this book is about...

How to read this book...

This book will change the way you perceive how you think. It it is designed to give you everything you need to change the way you think... FAST!

Each chapter contains anecdotes, stories, methods, and a play from the playbook that gives you a chance to practice the techniques contained in that chapter. Keep in mind, all of the exercises may not have enough space for your thoughts and ideas, so feel free to use the blank pages I've included for you at the end of each chapter or use an extra sheet of paper—the bigger the better. Make your ideas BIG, and post them on your walls so that you can revisit them frequently.

It is not enough to read the book—to think differently you have to complete the plays. If you merely read these plays, you will have no more than a suggestion on how to think differently.

Chapter 1
Think BIG!

Have you ever thought what your life will be like in ten years? Do you have ideas about your relationships, career, business, health, finances, and spirituality? We could probably take five days and fill up 50 flip charts with ideas of what you could do in your future. But really, investing that kind of creativity and time is a waste of energy. There just isn't any reason to generate stacks of ideas like that.

A better use of your time would be to ask yourself, "Of all the things I can work on, what are the three or four things that are really going to make a difference?" Instead of generating a lot of good ideas, you have to focus. There are so many good choices—but good is always the enemy of great. So you should focus on the three or four things that will make a difference.

How do you do that? You have to identify things that you can, want, and need to do. They have to be things you can get excited about—big things. Identify things that scare you, but are also aligned with who you are and who you want to be.

Are you ready to think BIG thoughts?

Have you ever wondered what results you could get if you allowed yourself to think big ... to think really BIG?

Have you found that you, your work team, or even your family wants to be different, yet they hold back. Sticking to phrases and excuses such as, "But this is how we've always done it!" or "We don't have the _____ (fill in the blank with time, money, talent, etc.) for that idea."

What if you could elevate your thinking?

During my trainings and keynotes, I like to encourage participants to stretch their thinking about changes they would like to see in both their personal and professional lives ... to think differently than they've always thought ... to think BIG!

While prepping for a training for a retail store's employee retreat, I stumbled upon the story below. As tears filled my eyes and threatened to overflow, I was reminded of how our thought process and frame of reference determine what we believe to be true—whether it is true or not.

Many years ago, when I worked as a volunteer at a hospital, I got to know a little girl named Liz who was suffering from a rare and serious disease. Her only chance of recovery appeared to be a blood transfusion from her five-year-old brother, who had miraculously survived the same disease, and had developed the antibodies needed to combat the illness.

The doctor explained the situation to her little brother, and asked the little boy if he would be willing to give his blood to his sister. I saw him hesitate for only a moment before taking a deep breath and saying, "Yes... I'll do it if it will save her life."

As the transfusion progressed, he lay in bed next to his sister and smiled, as we all did, seeing the color returning to her cheeks.

Then the little boy's face grew pale as he watched his sister, and his smile began to fade.

He looked up at the doctor and asked with a trembling voice, "Will I start to die right away?"

You see, his five-year-old thought process framed what he believed to be true. He thought he was going to have to give his sister **ALL** of his blood in order to save her.

Perception of reality is everything.

So the question is, what are you believing to be true, that in fact may not be based in truth? Is it time to think differently?

There are endless possibilities for real change and growth you can experience in your business or organization, or with your work team or family.

Think about how you currently do the following:

- Resolve conflicts
- Spend money
- Plan family meals
- Schedule exercise or active time
- Market your product or services
- Brand yourself through customer service
- Lead strategic planning
- Enhance team morale

Pick just one and now close your eyes or sit quietly and imagine the changes you would like to see. Imagine there are no obstacles and you are guaranteed that your ideas will succeed. Let your creativity go. Imagine BIG changes as well as little changes.

Begin your change imaginations with phrases such as:

- I wonder ...
- What if ...
- Imagine if we could ...

I wonder ... what strategic planning would look like this year if we took it off site, to someplace casual and relaxed, and hired a facilitator to come in to lead the process. Someone who knows how to motivate and inspire, as well as teach leaders and managers how to communicate to every employee in the organization. Then we will all have a core comprehension of how individual job performance affects successful execution of the plan.

What if ... you started a dinner co-op with two or three other families in your neighborhood? Each member of the co-op is responsible for one night's meal for all the families in the group. Keep track of who is cooking what, and when. A meal typically consists of a main course and two sides, and is dropped off at each member's house just before dinner so there is enough time to reheat it.

Imagine if we could ... truly create a culture of innovation. In this culture, employees make better decisions, begin to identify improvement opportunities, start to question the status quo and become a vital component of ongoing strategy discussions.

If your thoughts are big enough, you will not know how you will achieve everything when you start. Sure, you will have an idea of where to start, but not the whole picture. The "how" is not important right now; only the "what."

Having a lot of ideas is good, but now you have to find a way to simplify them or filter them down to what are really the most important ones for you.

The best way that I've learned to do that is to set up a "play" in the 3x3. Using the **Drill Down to the Future Matrix**, identify the ideas that are important to you for your future. It's a great way to take a lot of ideas and drill it down to the things that are important. The reason they're really important is because they are important to your future and your success, and they are things that you are not doing now.

FOCUS on a handful of ideas that will really make a difference.

IDENTIFY those ideas that are important for your future, but that you're not working on now. What were you thinking?

BIG thoughts should be unreasonable, if not, you are not thinking big enough. When you think big enough, it will challenge you and scare you at the same time.

George Bernard Shaw wrote "the reasonable man adapts himself to the world: the unreasonable one persists in trying to adapt the world to himself. Therefore all progress depends on the unreasonable man."

Thinking differently is easier said than done. And, almost anyone who consistently makes the effort to think differently CAN think differently. Once you learn how to do it, you'll find that you have some truly creative ideas and innovative solutions.

Think differently ... think BIG!

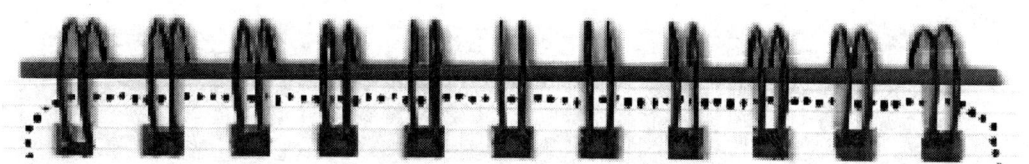

Drill Down to the Future

Make a list of all of your ideas about where you want to be one, three, or five years from now. What actions do you need to take to achieve each of those goals.

Then ask yourself, "How important is this item to my long-term success?" Each item should be labeled either Very Important, Important, or Not Important.

Now you can start plugging each item into the matrix on the following page. In the appropriate row—based on what you have identified as very important, important, or not important—think about each item and identify where are you now? Are you already doing it well and consistently; doing it, but not well or not consistently; or not doing it at all.

Write each of the ideas in the correct box in the matrix. In the top right-hand corner are the things that you have identified for your long-term success, but you are not doing anything about right now.

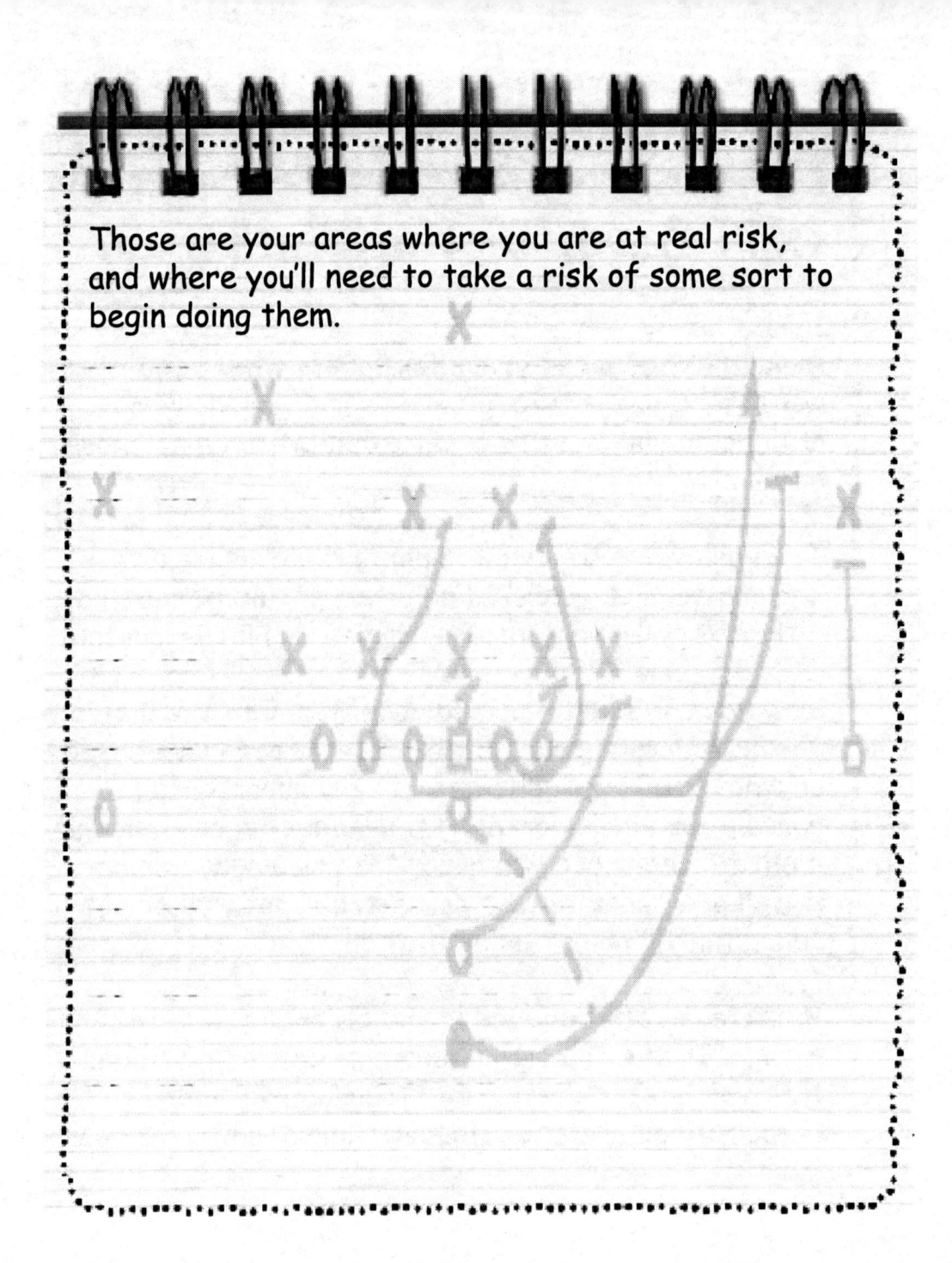

Those are your areas where you are at real risk, and where you'll need to take a risk of some sort to begin doing them.

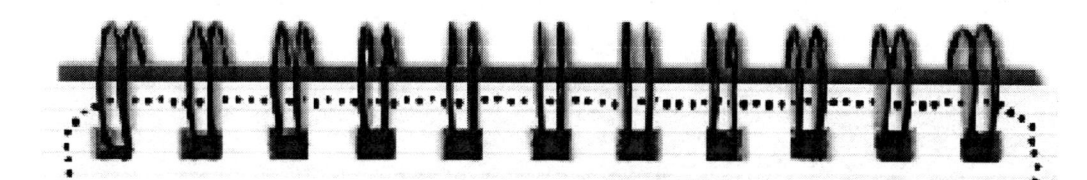

Where are you now?

	Already doing it well and doing it consistently.	Doing it, but struggling or not consistently.	Doing nothing about it.
Very Important			
Important			
Not Important			

How important is this to your long-term success?

Chapter 2
The Chubby Girl Factor

There are a set of theories that I call "Monica's Laws of the Universe." Granted, these theories are not based in science, or documented through scholarly research; they're just behaviors and results that I observe in family, friends, clients, colleagues, and even enemies.

One of the Laws is called **Greatest Fear – Greatest Success**. It states that your greatest area of fear—the thing you are most afraid of, the thing that causes your hands to get clammy and shake, your heart beat faster, and your stomach churn, whatever that is. Your greatest fear will be your ultimate area of success and triumph.

I believe, for example, that people who are terrified of getting in front of a group of people to speak really have something to say that others need to hear. Your main area of fear is more than likely the area where you are called to shine.

In every situation that you face, there is a filter that frames your perception of the world and the Law of Perception says, "You do not see the world as it really is, you see it as you perceive it to be."

Have you ever found yourself in a situation where you see someone who is successful and say, "I could never do that?" That kind of statement is based in fear or self-limiting belief.

Although I grew up with an athletic sister, I never saw myself as an athlete. Only 18 months older than me, people often compared us. My earliest memories involve comparisons of our looks, singing talents, brains, athleticism ... and weight.

I have an old black and white photo that became the main theme of my beliefs and habits. It shaped my childhood, teens, and most of my adult life. It is a picture of Melanie (my sister) and me. Melanie is about four and a half and I am three years old. In the picture we are facing each other; my sister has a pink and white gingham bikini with ruffles on the butt—cute, cute, cute! I, on the other hand, have on the ugliest navy blue tank suit you have ever seen.

> *It's always "Chubby girls CAN'T..." Never, "Chubby girls CAN..."*

The annoying thing is that my sister has no "fufu" in her at all. She could care less about those adorable ruffles on the butt.

I asked my mom if I could have a cute suit like Melanie's, and I was told that I was too "chubby" to wear a bikini. I needed to cover my belly and my thighs.

From the age of three, all my decisions were based on the belief that I was the chubby girl, and when you are the chubby girl, you make decisions based on the "chubby girl factor."

I learned that big and beautiful aren't ideas that go together. Chubby girls aren't the most popular, don't become cheerleaders, never date the hot guys, and aren't as smart as the thin, pretty girls.

I came to believe that I was not good enough, thin enough, smart enough, strong enough, or pretty enough. I only did those things that are appropriate for chubby girls to do—play an instrument in the band, sing in the choir, become a cast member in the musicals, earn straight B's, and serve as editor of the yearbook. I squashed many of my own desires, dreams, and ambitions because of these feelings of unworthiness.

Reality Check: Your fear or self-limiting beliefs may have nothing to do with being a chubby girl, but you've got something holding you back. Here are five of the most common self-limiting beliefs:

1. **Believing that you are not good enough:** You may believe you weren't born into the right family, the right race, the right gender, the right side of the tracks. Whatever reasons why you believe you aren't good enough, you use them to establish your belief about your abilities. Maybe someone said you weren't smart enough, that you don't have special abilities or qualities, or that you just need to do the "best that you can." The message is that you aren't smart enough, have no special qualities, that you aren't worthy to achieve great things.

2. **People just don't like me:** This is a big one a lot of people believe. Now I'm not talking about rude people; I'm talking about your basic nice person. This belief makes you think that no one wants to be your friend or would like you because of the flaws you have. The reality is we all have flaws, AND we are all likeable. People like people who like them. To have a friend, be a friend.

3. **I will be rejected.** We often don't put ourselves out there because we're afraid that people won't accept us. Maybe we don't offer our good idea because someone will criticize it. Or we might not make a suggestion for fear that people will scoff. One of the main reasons that sales people don't "ask for the sale" is because they are afraid they won't get it. They are afraid they will be told "No." The trouble is, if you don't ask, you don't get. Occasional rejection is better than being miserable. It's not worth limiting our experiences and contributions in life simply because of the possibility it won't be appreciated.

4. **Something is impossible to achieve.** Sometimes we give up too soon. We look at a task and assume we can't do what others have done. But most of the time, the reason it appears impossible is because we haven't learned yet how to make it possible. For example, I've been told by people who hear me speak that I am as good a speaker as the $25,000 keynoter they saw recently. Now, no one is paying me that kind of money, so evidently I'm not that

good of a speaker. It's not that I actually believe that it is impossible to get $25,000 to speak, it's just that I don't know how to make it happen. If I don't learn how, it is impossible. The same may be true for you. You accept that something isn't outside the range of possibility, but you don't know how to achieve your dream. If you don't know how to achieve your dream, study with the right people, read, learn, change mindsets. If you don't, it will be impossible to be successful.

5. **I am destined for failure.** This is one of the most damaging self-limiting beliefs that you can have, the belief that whatever you do will end up in failure. You may believe that if you try something, it is not going to work, so why bother. This belief could be why you haven't started or put much energy into the three or four things that you know will make the difference in achieving your dreams. Perhaps you are afraid of failing, or you believe that you will fail. You take on the view that if you don't do it, you can't fail. But if you think about it, aren't you failing by doing nothing?

As an adult I still fight that "chubby" label. I often take clothes into the dressing room that are way too large, but when eyeing up the smaller sizes, my belief is that I would never fit into them. It is amazing how the faulty belief system causes you to make certain decisions such as a career choice, fees charged to clients, even the friends, colleagues, and lovers you choose.

A couple years ago, for the first time in my life, I reached an athletic goal! I still am in disbelief that I did it—I ran 5 miles! Never in a million years would I have guessed that I could do it. I thought running was for other people, athletic people.

On Thanksgiving Day I ran the Austin Turkey Trot. I wasn't the fastest or sleekest runner out there, but I was OUT THERE.

Isn't that what life is all about? It's the times that we move past our fears and limiting beliefs that the magic happens. We smash the old mindsets and experience great rewards.

Yes, I was the "chubby sister" and Melanie the "thin, athletic sister." And that view has plagued me my whole life. But it no longer has to be my identity!

You too have words or thought patterns that have stayed with you your whole life. This kind of baggage weighs you down as you drag it around day after day.

It's like dragging a load of luggage through an airport. As you're running to catch your flight you think to yourself, "Why did I pack so much junk?" Yet, you walk around each day carrying a couple suitcases full of shame, fear, insecurities, and a distorted view of who you really are. It's torture, and you end up getting nowhere fast.

Why not shed a few of those limiting beliefs. You'll be fine without them. They are just keeping you from where you want to go. Perhaps more important, they are keeping you from giving your gift to the world.

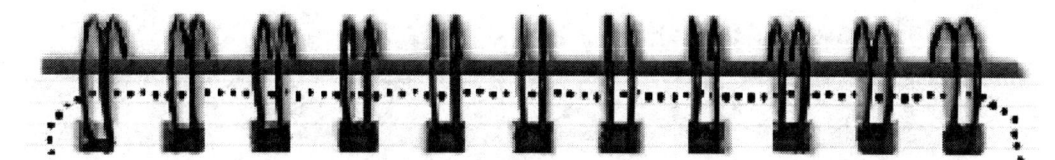

The Baggage Sweep

This will help you to unpack and start traveling a little lighter.

How to: Imagine that you are planning a trip to some fun or exotic location. What would you pack for such a trip? Swimsuit, shorts, jacket, etc? Just as if you were packing your bags to go on a trip, every morning you get up and pack an emotional suitcase.

Walk through each of the steps below to identify and release the emotional baggage that is holding you back from achieving all you want in life.

Step 1: Acknowledge It
For example a childhood disaster. Your parents weren't what you expected them to be, or situations that happened at school. Even if it wasn't a fairy-tale existence it is OK to acknowledge it.

Step 2: Own It
You may not have caused it, and you can blame it on whoever you like, but you won't move forward unless you own it. You have to wrap your arms around it and take personal responsibility.

Step 3: Get Someone to Help You Carry It
Talk to your family and friends about the excess baggage you've been carrying around. If you are holding a grudge find the person and apologize. Forgive others. And, if the bags are extremely heavy, you may need some professional help. If you continue to focus on the negative, you will be negative. Find the help you need.

Step 4: Move Forward and Pack Lighter!
Make a decision to leave the bags behind. Life is too short. Don't wear emotional baggage like it's a badge or cross you have to bear. Focus on the future and where you want to be.

It's time to unpack and get rid of the emotional baggage that has been holding you back. The more junk you unpack and get rid of from your past, the easier it will be to find the way toward the future you want.

You may never run five miles, but focus on finishing your race strong!

What kind of baggage do you carry around each day on the Trip of Life?

_____

_____

_____

_____

What do you have to do to own it? For example: What pain do you keep reliving? What negative feelings do you need to let go? What do you need to do to get emotional closure? Whom do you need to forgive?

_____

_____

_____

_____

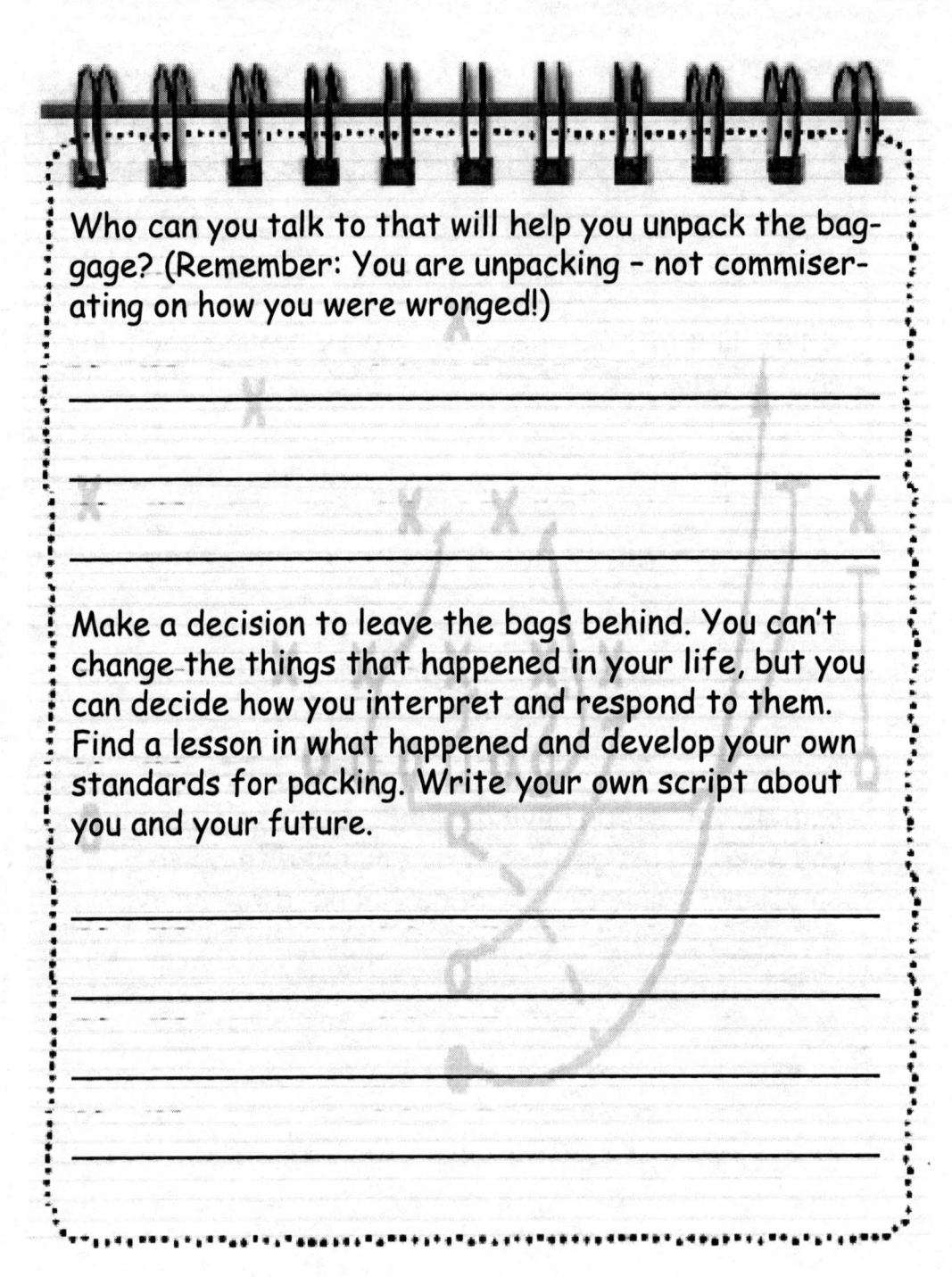

Who can you talk to that will help you unpack the baggage? (Remember: You are unpacking – not commiserating on how you were wronged!)

_____

_____

_____

Make a decision to leave the bags behind. You can't change the things that happened in your life, but you can decide how you interpret and respond to them. Find a lesson in what happened and develop your own standards for packing. Write your own script about you and your future.

_____

_____

_____

_____

Chapter 3
Ask the Right Questions

Imagine if you did not speak until you were four years old and didn't read until you were seven. What if your teachers described you as "mentally slow, unsociable and adrift forever in his foolish dreams." Do you know that is true for one of the greatest thinkers of all time? Have you heard of Albert Einstein?

Einstein said, "If I had an hour to solve a problem and my life depended on the solution, I would spend the first 55 minutes determining the proper question to ask, for once I know the proper question. I could solve the problem in less than five minutes."

How often do you spend time and resources on problems which don't necessarily demand such attention?

Too often our approach to problem solving is reactive; we wait for problems to arise.

The real starting point then for any problem solving process is to find the right problem to solve. Ask yourself, "Is it the right problem to solve?" and "What opportunities are created by this problem?"

Society teaches us that to see what is good in life is to be naïve, whereas to be critical is perceived to be informed, grounded, sophisticated, and grownup. This is why when we are looking at a situation and thinking of possibilities, we often focus on what is wrong and what can go wrong, instead of possibilities.

The consequence is that our thinking is usually based on an unbalanced and, therefore, incorrect picture.

Fear constricts everything, especially thinking. Thinking stops when we are upset. But if we express feelings just enough, thinking re-starts. Laughter actually improves thinking.

And did you know that you become smarter after a good cry?

Unfortunately, we have things backwards in our society. We think that when feelings start, thinking stops. And so when crying starts, for example, we try to stop the crying. When we do this, we interfere with exactly the process that helps a person to think clearly again.

So the next time a colleague or friend begins to show signs of feelings, relax and welcome them. Good thinking lies just around the corner.

Have you ever thought about how you make decisions? Do you end up in "trouble" because your choices left the people around you asking, "What were you thinking?"

The truth is, you probably weren't thinking; you were just acting on an instinct or used some kind of mental shortcut to reach your decision.

Chances are, you weren't asking the right questions to get the right answer.

Let me illustrate with a story about my son Nick, his grandfather, and the conversation I overheard one morning while Pap-Pap was making breakfast for Nick.

Pap-Pap prepared a big bowl of oatmeal, his own favorite breakfast.

"Do you like sugar?" Pap-Pap asked Nick.

Nick nodded yes.

"How about some butter, too?"

Again Nick nodded yes.

"Of course, you like milk?"

"Sure," Nick replied.

> *Warning: The easy answer isn't always the right one*

But when Pap-Pap placed the steaming bowl of oatmeal with butter, sugar, and milk before him, Nick refused to eat it.

His Pap-Pap was exasperated. "But Nick when I asked you, didn't you say you liked sugar, butter, and milk?"

"Yes," replied Nick, "But Pap-Pap, you didn't ask me if I liked oatmeal."

As this story shows, the way you ask a question can greatly influence the answer you get.

The same is true for every decision you make, or problem you solve. If you frame your problem poorly, you're unlikely to make a smart choice.

Typically when faced with an uncertainty, we don't carefully evaluate the information or look for facts and statistics. Instead, in making decisions we use biases and shortcuts that are hardwired into our thinking process. These shortcuts can be dangerous because they create blind spots. So we fail to recognize what lies in our blindspots, and fall into a trap of faulty thinking.

Daniel Kahneman in his book, *Thinking, Fast and Slow*, gives a great example of this. Answer this simple arithmetic question: A bat and ball together cost $1.10. The bat costs a dollar more than the ball. How much does the ball cost?

If you are like most people, you respond quickly and confidently, and tell me that the ball costs ten cents.

Well that answer is both obvious and wrong. (The correct answer is five cents for the ball and a dollar and five cents for the bat.)

Your answer used some mental shortcuts. These shortcuts aren't a faster way of doing the math; they're a way of skipping the math altogether.

At every stage of your decision making process you run into misconceptions, inaccurate frames of reference, biases, and other blind spots that can distort the choices you make.

Inc. Magazine has called Doug Hall "America's top new idea man." Hall, a self-styled inventor, entrepreneur, and author, helps companies build their businesses with new ideas and strategies. I first read his books while working on my Masters program in economic development and entrepreneurship.

Hall is the founder and CEO of Eureka! Ranch, which is a corporate innovation, research and training center. His big name clients include American Express, AT&T, Johnson & Johnson, Mattel, and Pepsi-Cola, to name just a few.

Hall says to be successful with Innovation Engineering there are three simple things you must embrace:

1. **I Don't Know** (meaning you are open to learning more)

2. **I Need Help** (meaning you are open to asking for help, and to diversify your thinking with those inside and outside your organization)

3. **I Love to Learn from Failing** (meaning you seek to *Fail FAST and Fail CHEAP*)

The barrier to these three simple things (I don't know, I need help, and I love to learn from failing) is the unhealthy ego. We feel the need to protect ourselves, to make sure others don't find us lacking or stupid. But the truth is by avoiding these three things, we actually look stupid and make bad decisions.

Instead, a healthy ego admits that we don't know everything. We become aware that taking a risk and opening ourselves up is actually a sign of strength—not weakness.

- Henry Ford failed and went broke five times before he finally succeeded.

- Thomas Edison discovered thousands of ways not to make a light bulb.

- Walt Disney was fired by a newspaper editor for lack of ideas. Disney also went bankrupt several times before he built Disneyland.

Imagine how our lives would have been different if these men had not learned from their failures. What about the countless other people who had a similar work ethic and who didn't fear failure?

When you embrace that you don't know everything, that you need help, and when you love to learn from failing, you actually become smarter.

This process starts with asking questions and openly sharing your fears, successes, failures, and risks.

What techniques and strategies are you using to help ensure that the way you are framing a problem doesn't prevent you from solving it? Are you asking the right questions to get the right answers?

The next play will help you change the way you think... quickly.

Right Questions Run

Write down your thoughts for each of the next three steps and the move you will make for each.

Step 1: Ask, "What don't I know?"
This week ask and admit you don't know something. Then become a learner. Start with the Internet, the bookstore, the library, or a friend—the answers to most of the world's problems are there. You just need to be open to learning.

_____

_____

_____

_____

_____

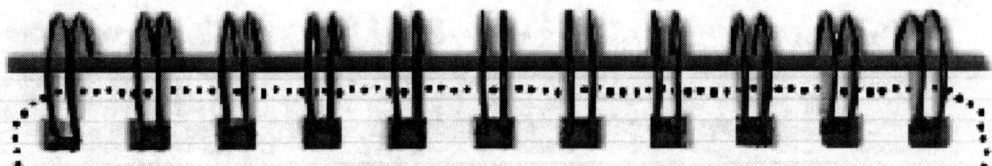

Step 2: Ask, "I'm wondering if you can help me." This week admit and ask for the help you need. Then diversify your thinking by asking for help with those outside your organization or immediate circle of influence. Most successful people will help you if you ask them. Value their time and pay them for it if necessary.

_____

_____

_____

_____

_____

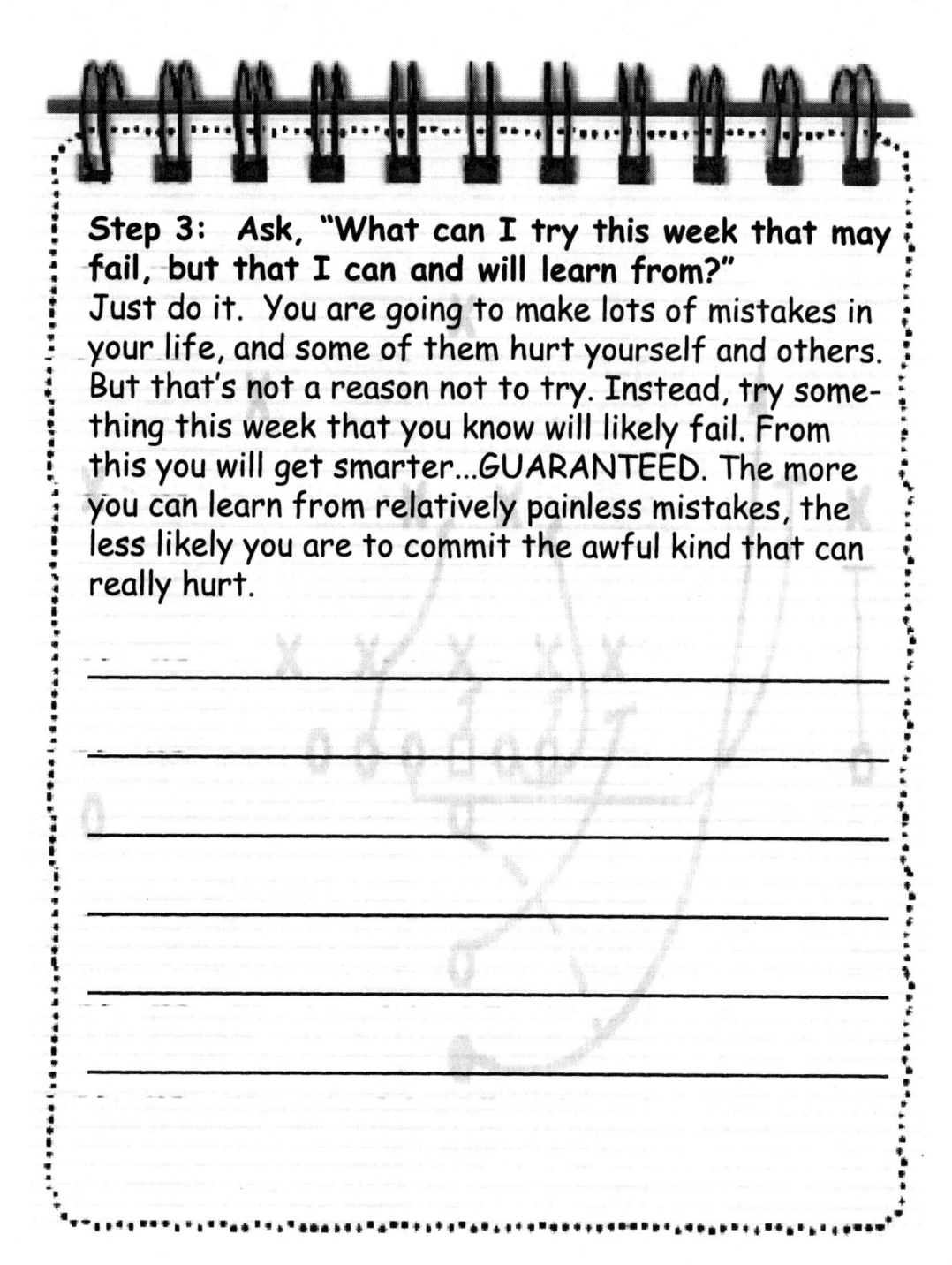

Step 3: Ask, "What can I try this week that may fail, but that I can and will learn from?"

Just do it. You are going to make lots of mistakes in your life, and some of them hurt yourself and others. But that's not a reason not to try. Instead, try something this week that you know will likely fail. From this you will get smarter...GUARANTEED. The more you can learn from relatively painless mistakes, the less likely you are to commit the awful kind that can really hurt.

_____

_____

_____

_____

_____

_____

Let me add a couple more questions to round out this play.

What am I pretending not to know?
All possibilities open up when we stop deceiving ourselves. For example, do you really not know how to save money, lose weight, have a more loving relationship? If you really don't know, then go back up to Steps 1, 2, and 3 above and figure it out. If you do know, then after writing them down in the space provided, continue to the next question.

_____

_____

_____

_____

_____

_____

Why don't I do the things I know I should be doing?

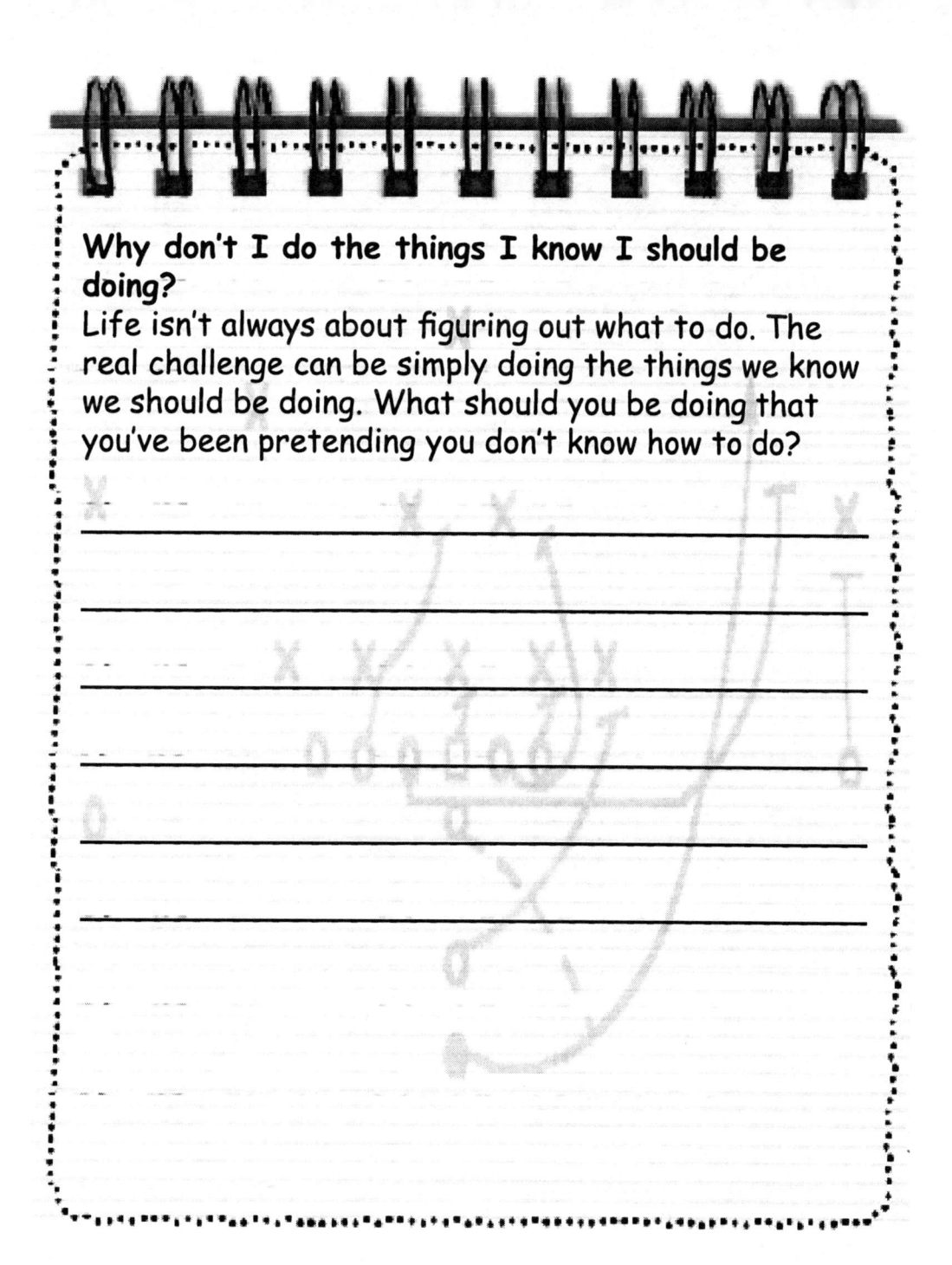

Life isn't always about figuring out what to do. The real challenge can be simply doing the things we know we should be doing. What should you be doing that you've been pretending you don't know how to do?

_____

_____

_____

_____

_____

Chapter 4
Drop the F Bomb

There is a four-letter word that begins with "F," and you are not supposed to mention it in public. People are shocked and surprised when you do say it. You can see the disapproval in their eyes when you say it. They may even rebuke you with, "What were you thinking? I can't believe you said that!"

No, not *that* "F" word—I'm talking about FEAR. Something that everyone has, yet seldom will you hear anyone admit to it.

There are certain speakers in my network who have a certain bravado or reputation, and who have achieved an envious level of success. Yet I know, even they have fear. In a world that is changing so rapidly and an economy that is still not predictable, fear is natural and even considered normal. In fact, if you aren't having some anxiety, you are probably playing it too safe.

What makes fear so powerful and potent is that it is self-fulfilling as well as self-reinforcing. Fear can create the very thing you are afraid of. And once it is triggered, it tends to gather momentum, thus confirming your fear.

If you don't feel any nervousness or anxiety, you have probably been doing what you are doing for too long, and that in itself is a reason to have fear.

Have you heard the saying, "If you aren't standing on the edge, you are taking up too much space?" You've got to be standing on that edge, ready to take a risk. Occasionally we can excel when we are afraid, when that fear comes and the adrenaline is pumping. But most often, fear prevents you from performing at your peak. It causes many of the mistakes that ruin the quality of your work and that, ultimately, ruin the quality of your life.

I remember when I did my very first keynote speech. The group hiring me wanted a 30 minute motivational session, and they had a $2,000 budget. Needless to say, I was thrilled to contract the engagement with them.

The morning of the event I wasn't so excited. As I sat in my hotel room reviewing my notes, I started the negative self-talk that sounded something like this, "What were you thinking? What are you doing? These people booked you because of your *Lipstick* book. They don't even know you. They are paying you $2,000 for 30 minutes. What could you possibly say in 30 minutes that would be worth that money?"

> *Fear and self-limiting beliefs create more fear and self-limiting beliefs*

And then, because negative self-talk builds momentum, I began thinking, "Well, then if you don't have anything to say in 30 minutes for $2,000, what about when a group offers to pay you $5,000? Or $10,000? If you don't think you have anything worthwhile to say now, how will it be then?"

I was talking myself out of leaving the hotel room. I wanted to stay there and skip the luncheon altogether.

The two greatest enemies that stop your dreams are the fear and self-limiting beliefs that fill you with more fear and self-limiting beliefs.

Fear can make you deviate from your intended path of success. Self-limiting beliefs can diminish and even destroy your hopes and dreams. They cause you to look at the negative and lose focus on what you really want. In the end, you tell yourself, "I can't do that! What was I thinking?"

It is just amazing how this works. Fear and self-limiting beliefs act like brakes and keep you from achieving your goals. You're moving forward, and all of a sudden fear and self-limiting beliefs pop their heads up. That's when the brakes come on, causing you to stop instead of moving forward. You are then incapable of taking the intelligent risks necessary to achieve your desires and fulfill your potential.

I'm sure there is a gap between where you are and where you want to be. Could it be that fear and self-limiting beliefs are widening this gap?

That gap is the risks you haven't taken. The thing is, to get to the next level, you must cross that gap. But as you attempt to cross it, fear and self-limiting beliefs act like a rubber band, pulling you back. You try to reach that next level, but the elasticity of that rubber band pulls you right back to your comfort zone. Inside the comfort zone there is no room for courage, boldness, or enthusiasm, only comfort, status quo, and discouragement.

Your dreams are killed, and the prophecy is fulfilled.

Let's walk through the fear cycle together.

Phase one is an imagined consequence. You imagine the situation turning catastrophic. You turn the situation into an absolute calamity where the worst possible consequences are imagined.

Before that first keynote, I saw myself tripping up the steps to the stage, sprawled out spread eagle, in a skirt no less!

Since the negative thoughts are flowing, you lose your perspective. The more ambiguous or uncertain you are in that setting, the more room there is for negative thinking.

Remember when you were a kid lying in your bed at night, and the things in the shadows weren't clear and everything became scary? Even to this day my sister won't sleep with either her hands or her feet hanging over the edge of the bed because of the fear of the monster under the bed. She's over 50 years old, and she still can't have her feet or hands over the bed.

But she's not abnormal. We all have irrational fears that continue. We imagine monsters, calamities, and the worst that could ever possibly happen, even when the likelihood is so remote it would boggle a statistician.

Phase two kicks in and distorts your perspective. Have you heard of people who wear rose-colored glasses? Everything looks beautiful through those lenses. Fear is like that only with the opposite effect. Instead of rose-colored glasses you look through gray or dark lenses that distort what you see, and make everything worse than it is.

Recently I was hired by a client to write a webinar. The topic was a real stretch for me, and I put extra hours into research and content writing. When the first draft of the script came back to me with suggested edits, I immediately thought, "Oh my, you can't make this happen. You don't measure up. You've disappointed them. You can't write this webinar! What were you thinking?"

The script weighed 200 pounds in my hands. I dropped it on my kitchen counter and walked away. Then, about 30 minutes later, I came back and read through their notes. I realized the changes they were asking for were minimal. Just a little more thought, a little more effort, to get the webinar to the level they wanted it to be.

> *"I'll do it later," means, "I won't do it."*

In other words, what we think is a catastrophe, may be a simple hurdle. The consequences may be much smaller than they look. Our distortions make it worse than it is.

Then the body signals start coming. Physical responses to fear like shortness of breath, dry mouth, shaking hands, and butterflies begin overwhelming us once we feel out of control.

When you are looking through those gray and dingy glasses that distort reality, you see and hear the very things that you are trying to avoid.

When I read the revision notes for that webinar, I failed to see the dozen of comments that said "Oh this is great," "Love this analogy," "This is wonderful, great way to expand that." I didn't see them at all.

I only saw comments like "Give me an example here." Or, "Let's expand this a little more." These were not negative comments, but fear and gray-colored glasses distorted them. What overwhelmed me was actually very encouraging. But my body responses acted as if I were in real danger. They caused me to shut down and run away. If I had not been afraid, I would have read the comments for what they were.

Another response to fear is procrastination. Somewhere in your head is the hope that if you put off what seems too hard or too scary, it will go away or get easier.

Have you ever said, "I do my best work under pressure. When the deadline is there that is when the creativity flows, that's when I do my best work?"

Even while you're saying this, you know that it is nonsense.

When you are in that do-or-die mode, you will not perform at your best, no matter what you say. When you're stressed, you can't concentrate. You can't think straight. You lose all hope of creativity.

Fear will compromise your performance, and it is at that point that you enter the final phase of fear, which is concrete confirmation of what you were afraid of. What you feared becomes your reality, a self-fulfilling prophecy.

Since most of our fears and self-limiting beliefs are automatic, they kick in before we have a chance to even think about them. It's time to challenge those fears and self-limiting beliefs because:

If you change your thinking, you change your beliefs. And when you change your beliefs, you change your life.

In the book *Habits Die Hard*, authors Anderson and Murphy reference a practice from Buddhist teacher, James Barasz, that you can use to dispel fear and limiting beliefs, even when you think you can't. It's called **RAIN**: Recognize, Accept, Investigate, Non-identify.

Recognize: Become aware of what is going on. Write down what is going on right now.

_____

_____

_____

_____

_____

_____

_____

Accept: Rather than thinking negative thoughts and shaming yourself, accept with graciousness what is going on.

_____

_____

_____

_____

_____

Investigate: What feelings are you experiencing? What body signals or physical responses? (shortness of breath, dry mouth, shaking hands, butterflies, etc.)

_____

_____

_____

_____

Non-identify: Tell yourself, "These thoughts and feelings are not me. They are passing through. I am more than these thoughts and feelings. I can choose not to respond." How will you non-identify?

_____

_____

_____

_____

_____

Now the work starts. What changes will you make now that you have identified these things? How will you non-identify with your fears and self-limiting beliefs. They are there, but they don't need to be. All you have to do is look at them, acknowledge them, and move beyond them.

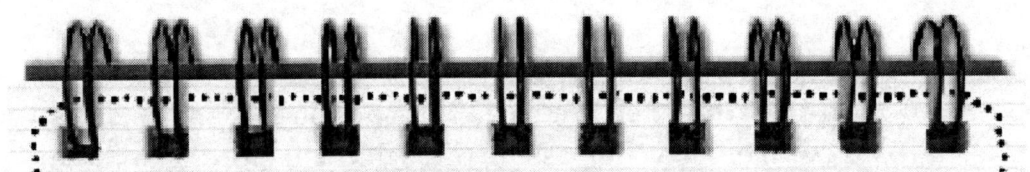

Drop the F Bomb

Answer these questions as honestly as you can - don't try to come up with the "right" answers; there are none. Write down whatever comes into your head when you read the questions.

What am I meant to be doing with my life?

_____
_____
_____

Looking back at my life, I wish I had:

_____
_____
_____

Looking back at my life, I wish I hadn't:

_____

_____

_____

How could I have done things better?

_____

_____

_____

What can I change about my actions in the future?

_____

_____

_____

When I think of failure my fears include?

_____

_____

_____

When I think of success my fears include?

_____

_____

_____

If I couldn't fail, I would:

_____

_____

_____

If I could add anything to my life right now, it would be:

_____

_____

_____

If I could remove anything from my life right now, it would be:

_____

_____

_____

Chapter 5
DNF is Not an Option

How do you stop the cycle of fear and limiting beliefs? Unfortunately, there is no pill you can take that will eliminate doubt, fear, and limiting beliefs. Wouldn't it be great if there were? Instead of a pill to lose weight while you sleep, you could take a pill to lose your fear, doubt, and self-limiting beliefs while you sleep.

But no, we must face our fears and limited beliefs on our own. There isn't a quick way through them.

It is important to understand that no one else can make you overcome those feelings; you have to do it on your own. Sometimes when others try to help, they actually make it worse.

I sometimes get really nervous before a big speaking engagement, and my friends tell me, "Don't worry, you'll do great!" As much as I appreciate my friends and their encouraging words, the words don't mean anything unless I believe them too.

It's the same with you. Unless you believe the positive, words of encouragement won't do any good.

Professional counselors and coaches can help you understand what may be causing the fear and limiting beliefs, but the main transformation has to come from you. The change has to happen in your mind.

Here is a proven strategy to cut fear down to size:

First, do a "reality check." Weigh the fear. How bad is it on a scale from 1 to 10? Assess what is really true about this situation and your ability to deal with it. Almost all fear is exaggerated and irrational.

Next, do a "worst case scenario" exercise. What is the worst that can happen?

A few years back, my then-husband and I were going through a major job transition, and I was scared. What are we going to do about jobs? How are we going to pay our bills? Where are we going to live? I exaggerated the whole situation to the point that I envisioned us living under a bridge... in a box... with our cat.

Then we did a reality check and went through the worst case scenarios. Yes, we might have to live in an apartment for awhile. If that is the worst case scenario, I can live with that. If fact, if you think about it, that can be better than the hassle of a house with land.

The reality is, if you can live with the worst case scenario, then it's probably okay for you to take the risk and act on what you want to do. If you aren't prepared to live with the worst case scenario, then perhaps it's better to put your idea on a shelf for awhile until you are better prepared.

You need to be aware of your thoughts and be the master of them. You can develop your mind to be stronger, so you can challenge your own self-defeating beliefs. If you want to get out of that self-limiting place, you've got to move forward. The first step can be scary, but when you realize that the worst case is not really that bad, it becomes easier to face an uncertain future.

To feel good about yourself, you have to achieve or be successful at something. So why not take the steps that will create success? Move forward on something, and you will have success. That success will prepare you for more risk and more success. You just have to determine to take that first step.

> *What's the worst that could happen? This is probably not that bad.*

Reject the negative thoughts when they appear, such as, "What were you thinking? You can't do this. You're not smart enough, or good enough or _____ enough" (fill in the blank). You have to change that mindset and say that you are talented, you are capable, and then focus on whatever it is you desire to do.

The reality is the person you have the most conversations with is yourself. What kinds of things are you saying? You would probably never talk to other people the way you talk to yourself. You would never tell anyone "You are such a loser. What were you thinking?"

So turn those words around. But understand that you can't just stop the negative thoughts because that creates a vacuum; you've got to replace them with positive words. If you don't have a set of affirmations written out, I would recommend that you start writing out things like:

"The world needs me. I need to get out there."

"I was put here for a reason, and I need to do what I am called to do so somebody else is able to do what they are called to do."

"People like me and want to bless me."

I say phrases like this over and over because at times the chubby girl fear comes back and threatens to keep me from doing what I need and want to do.

I remember when I was a teenager. One day after school, I came home and grabbed a snack. I had a carrot in one hand and a bottle of Tab in the other. My mom looked at me, horrified, and said, "What are you eating?"

"Mom, it's a carrot and a Tab." I was thinking there are zero calories here. I can't believe she's freaking out.

But for her, she saw the chubby girl eating... again. I don't say this to be mean or complain. She was doing what she thought was best... worrying about me eating and gaining weight.

When I was around 15, I was doing a lot of exercise and really watching what I ate. One morning at breakfast, I said to my dad, "Hey Dad, I lost five pounds!"

My Dad's response was, "Hey Monica, turn around. I think I found it."

He was joking, of course. But those kinds of words hurt and stay around for a long time. He didn't realize he was perpetuating the chubby girl image and frame of reference.

People may have said negative things to you that created a frame of reference that persists in your adult life. On the other hand, you might have been protected from negative words when you were young. Maybe you developed a frame of reference that was created by only positive words.

I love my friend Gay. She is so tenacious. When anyone would say something negative about her kids, she'd cut them off mid-sentence and say, "Stop! I'm not going to let you curse my kids." Wow! Talk about creating a positive frame of reference.

> *Not quitting takes determination*

We have to be that conscientious about the words that are being spoken over us and who we associate with. You have to get around positive people.

If you want to break out of fear and limiting beliefs, you've got to take it into your own hands. Ignore the people who put you down. Perhaps a relationship needs to be terminated. I'm not saying to treat anyone badly, but there are people who should not be in your close circle of friends. You might want to keep them around to prove them wrong, but prove them wrong from a distance.

Be bold. Mix with uplifting people who have done more than you, who make more money than you, who are more creative or have more experience than you because that is how you are going to get better.

Yes, it takes some guts to reach out to these people. But understand, if you are the brightest person in the room, than you are running with the wrong pack. Yeah, it might make you feel good to be the brightest, smartest, richest, or best-looking in the room, but that is the furthest you will ever go. You won't be able to rise above where you are. Instead, if you really want to achieve in life, you have to get around people who can take you to the next level.

Recently when I was in Hawaii, my adventure-seeking friend said, "Let's climb to the top of Diamond Head!"

I immediately got online to see what climbing to the top of Diamond Head looks like. The description said things like, "76 steps straight up, and then 90 more steps straight up." The entire description was up, up, up.

It created a lot of fear. What if I'm not able to finish? What if it is too tough for me?

I don't do heights well. I'm that person at the top of the escalator, hanging on to the rails, with one foot out, waiting, then pulling back, then out again, until finally I just make myself plant a foot on the damn escalator.

I did the same thing with Diamond Head. I hesitated, but then said, "Just climb the damn mountain."

But what the advertising failed to mention is that once you get all the way up, almost to the very top, there is a double set of spiral staircases that take you to the peak.

When I reached these staircases, I panicked. My breathing was shallow and nausea set in. There was a swarm of people behind me and in front of me. I had nowhere to go but up.

So, I grabbed that rail and I said "Get going!" And I made it to the top! The views of the island are amazing from all the way up there! I'm so glad I pushed through. And now the views from atop the mountain are some of the best memories I have.

You might think that my fear and struggle is the silliest thing you've ever heard. But I know you've got your own stuff that may seem silly to me. There are monsters hiding under your bed.

The important thing to remember is reframing our language allows us to fill our heads with the positive rather than the negative. When we do, the benefits are enormous.

Remember the Turkey Trot I ran? It was one of the hardest things I have ever done in my life. But I was determined that I was going to finish.

I had trained for the race. I was ready ... or so I thought.

At about the 3.5 mile point, I started having doubts about whether I was going to be able to make it to the finish line.

If you haven't run a race, or paid attention to the postings that come afterward, you may not know that when someone drops out of a race, they post "DNF," or Did Not Finish.

When I started to falter, I began talking sharply to myself. I said, "Do you really want a DNF after your name? What does that say about you?"

I told myself that quitting was not an option. I would not have a DNF after my name, not for that race or in my life.

Poet John Milton wrote, "The mind is its own place and in itself, can make a Heaven of Hell, or a Hell of Heaven." Is your mind making a heaven or a hell, for you?

Here are a couple of examples of how you can turn your negative words (and the accompanying self-defeating thoughts) into positive communication (and self-empowering actions):

> Instead of saying, "That's just the way I am."
> Say, "I have decided to try a different approach."
> This keeps you in control of your future.
>
> Instead of saying you have a "problem."
> Call it an "opportunity."
> This allows for a self-empowering improvement of the situation.
>
> Instead of saying, "I have to…"
> Say "I choose to."
> This lets you take back the power.

Always reframe your language so that you have control over what you do and who you are.

Can you make a commitment to focus on this for 30 days? Every time a negative thought tries to enter your head, banish it, reframe it, and replace it with a positive thought. After 30 days, reframing will become your new habit.

DNF is not an option. You have to finish. Even if you've made mistakes in the past, it's time to unpack those bags of doubt and unbelief and finish strong.

DNF is Not an Option

Things I want to do.		
What is the risk? How bad is it really on a scale of 1-10		
Worst Case Scenario What is the worst thing that can happen?		
Can I live with the worst case scenario?		
Action Steps I choose to take.		

Chapter 6
FUNK in Your TRUNK

You go through your life following the patterns you've grown comfortable with. You do things because that's the way they're done. Your routine seems so natural that it doesn't even occur to you that you're following patterns at all.

You overlook opportunities, or fail to see warning signs, because you've kept your eyes not on the target, but on the routine. It happens to all of us.

Yet, have you found that **change is inevitable, and growth is optional?**

You may wonder why does this or that happen all the time. You may ask, "Why do I have so much resistance to change?"

Well it's because of the FUNK.

The box on the next page represents your life. It's everything you know, everything you've experienced, all the skills that you have developed, and all the feelings that you have ever felt.

You are living inside that box. Anytime you want to make a change to do something different you run into what I call **FUNK**... **F**ear, **U**ncertainty, **N**egativity, and **K**now it Alls.

If you want to make a change, you have to get outside the box because the box is what got you here. It won't get you there.

Yet as you try to get outside the box, you run into the edges. Those edges threaten to keep you inside the box. Whenever you try to do what you haven't done, you will run into:

Fear – "What if I fail? What will people say about me?" or "What if there's repercussions for trying to do something differently?"

Uncertainty - You hope and dream that things are going to be better outside your box, but what if you get out there and discover it really isn't better?

Negativity – Those thoughts that run through your head that say you don't really have what it takes. You aren't smart, creative, talented, or experienced enough.

Know it Alls – The people who tell you things like, "That's not the way we do it around here." "Leadership will never go for it." "I don't think it's worth the risk."

Here are a couple things to understand about FUNK. Everybody has it! I call it ***FUNK in your TRUNK***.

No matter how pulled together someone looks, they've got FUNK. Some people have learned how to unpack their FUNK, and they are driving those little tiny Smart cars. Others

Draw a picture of you in the box below. This is you inside your FUNK.

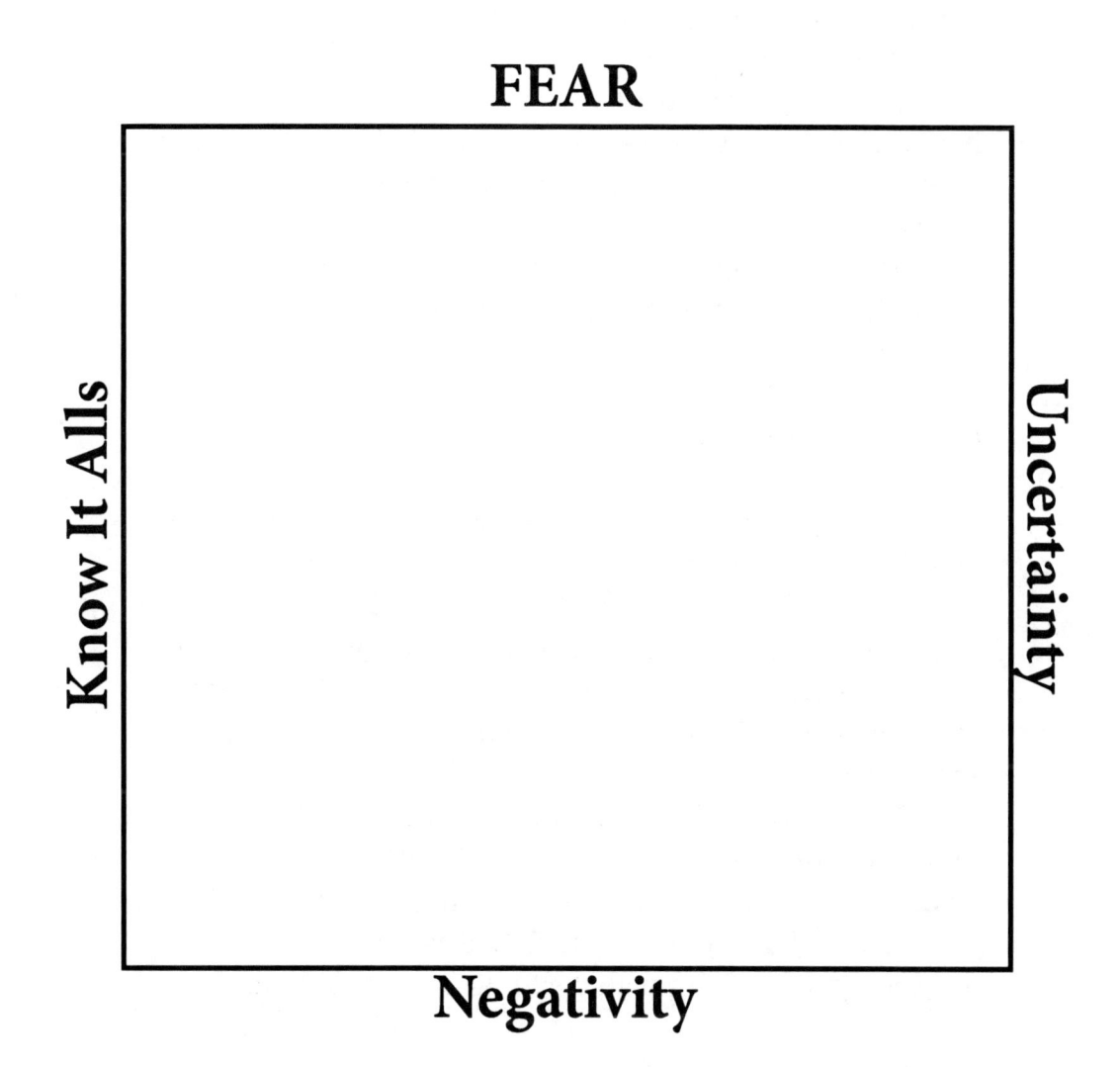

FEAR

Know It Alls

Uncertainty

Negativity

are pulling a whole 18-wheel tractor-trailer behind them full of FUNK.

Do you have those perfect friends? They have the perfect house, perfect spouse, perfect kids, perfect pets, and they take perfect vacations.

Then they send you the Christmas letter to tell you just how perfect their year was. Have you read that letter and thought, "Oh my gosh! We are such losers. Look at this family. They are perfect!"

Well, I'm thinking there's probably some FUNK in their trunk if they have to write a letter to you to tell you how perfect they are.

It makes things a whole lot easier when you realize that everybody has FUNK.

When you want to try something new, to get out of those patterned routines that you follow, there are a few pitfalls to avoid making it easier to fight through the FUNK.

The first is trying to solve today's problems with yesterday's solutions. Yesterday's solutions work until they don't work anymore. When you want something new, yesterday's solutions aren't going to work.

The second is viewing mistakes as failures. When you're in that box and you decide to try something new, chances are good that the first time out it's not going to work exactly as you planned. If every mistake is viewed as a failure, how often will you try to break through the funk to try something new?

Things are changing faster and faster, and there's no slowing in sight. The bottom line is you can either lead the change or be collateral damage as the change rolls over you.

You can't expect yourself or other people to be great without making mistakes. In fact, failure should be expected. It's been said, if you never fail, you are not trying hard enough.

The key to success in the face of change is to identify failure as quickly as possible. Fast failure is acceptable; slow failure is not. Failing quickly means finding a successful alternative quickly before the failure causes too much damage. In most cases you can find another approach, another process, another solution that will work.

This requires two standard rules of practice.

The first is to accept mistakes and failure as part of the process. If you get upset every time you are given bad news, then bad news will not be delivered to you. It is critical that you understand why failure occurred. And you must be willing to discuss what went wrong and what could have been done better. After all, what good is the failure to you if you don't learn from it?

The second is to encourage creative, outside-the-lines thinking. Some people believe that you are born creative. It's not true. Yes, some have advantages over others in this area, but new thinking habits can be nurtured and developed in yourself and others.

When there is failure, embrace it. Get creative. Creativity is experimenting, taking risks, breaking rules, making mistakes, and having fun.

The last pitfall to avoid when dealing with FUNK is an intolerance for risk. When you try something new, there's always risk involved.

To make it easier to take risks, you need to be really clear on what it is you want, and what the outcome is you're looking for.

When you stay in the box because of FUNK, everything will look the exact same way, the same patterns, and same routines.

Outside the box is where new things happen. Until you can fight through the FUNK and get to the other side, you'll keep getting the same old things. Outside the box, there is a whole new world, but inside you'll only see the same things over and over.

Remember... change is inevitable, growth is optional.

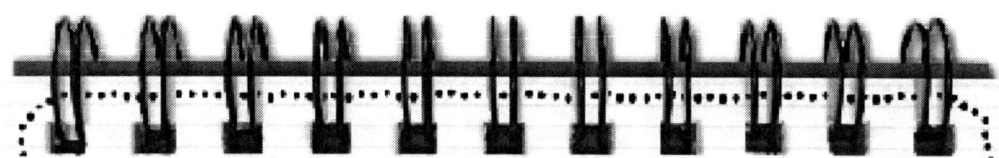

Fight the FUNK

START	Things that would be beneficial for me to START doing.
STOP	Things I'm currently doing that are not working and I should STOP doing them.
CONTINUE	Things I am currently doing well that I should CONTINUE doing.

Chapter 7
Where is Your North?

As a professional speaker, I occasionally get to travel with other speakers for a conference or series of workshops. A couple years ago, I travelled for two weeks with Janice for a series of women's conferences.

Although we had never met, I had heard very nice things about Janice. I called her a couple days before we were scheduled to meet, so we could chat and get to know each other.

I liked Janice instantly. But toward the end of the conversation she said to me, "By the way, I want to let you know that I like to run a really tight budget when I'm traveling. So, I don't like to spend a lot of money on food. I would prefer that we just do fast food most nights. Maybe we can plan to sit down and have one nice meal together during the week."

I thought… "Yuck!!! Fast Food! I don't like that idea. It doesn't sound very healthy nor fun."

Not sure how to respond I said, "Uh, uh. OK that sounds fine. We can do that."

After I hung up, I started to get frustrated. Eating fast food every night is not the best choice for me. I thought, "Why does she get to set the schedule? She's not the boss of me. She can't tell me what I'm going to eat. I'm probably not going to like her at all!"

And so, although I had said her plan was OK, I had real resistance inside of me.

The second or third night of our week together, we had a 100 mile drive to our next city, and Janice started telling me a little bit more about her life, her family, and her goals.

She said that within three years, she and her husband planned to retire. And it was their goal to have a home on the Big Island of Hawaii. Their plan was to live in that house six months out of the year, and then live close to their grandkids the other six. She said, "So that is why I am so frugal when I am on a speaking swing. ALL of our financial decisions are based on the goal of getting that new house."

She then added, "The great thing is, we are not going to be there six months out of the year. Our plan is to put the house into some kind of rental pool for our friends and family at a really super discounted rate."

I looked over at my new *BEST* friend and asked her, "Janice, which fast food restaurant would you like to eat at tonight?"

Wow! Many of us have goals just like Janice. How many of us walk that goal back step-by-step to determine how much we will spend on eating out each week? Instead, we make excuses that sacrifice our long term goals for our short term gratification. We think that somehow things will get better, even if we do everything the same way we've always done it.

True North is a winning play from the playbook that I often use in my Strategic Thinking Workshops. It is a set up for turning ideas into a plan that will give direction and offer a unified vision.

I ask the audience to stand and to stick their right arm out straight in front of them, pretending that their arm is the needle of a compass and their body is the compass.

Now, with their eyes closed and without looking around, I have them turn and point in the direction that they think is True North.

After everyone has chosen a direction, I have them open their eyes. Of course, everyone is pointing in a different direction. I then ask them if this is what their team looks like.

The reason this play is such an important one in the playbook is that you (and anyone else with you) can visibly see how important it is to know where your north is. Your north is where you are going—your vision. In order to get there, or to lead a family, team, or organization there, you must know where north is and get everyone going in the same direction.

Janice knows exactly where her North is, and she has calculated the steps necessary to reach it.

Let me give you six simple questions you can ask and answer that will help you to find Your North and also drill down to exactly when, where, and how you will get there:

Where are you now?

Remember the last time you were lost. Your GPS is no help. All she keeps saying is "recalculating." Finally in frustration you call your friend and say, "I'm lost! I don't know how to get to your house." What is the very first question they ask you? They say, "Where are you now?" Why? Because they can't tell you how to get to their house if they don't know where you are.

    The same is true when you are trying to determine where you want to go, you can't map your route if you don't know where you're starting from.

_____

_____

_____

_____

Where do you want to go?
Where is your North? Janice was so set on her North (buying that house in Hawaii) that she didn't let things throw her off course.

_____

_____

_____

_____

_____

How will you get there?
Which is the best route to take and how can you avoid a roadblock or construction zones that will slow you down? Is there an alternative route that you might take?

_____

_____

_____

_____

How will you know you're there?
Have you heard the phrase, "If you can't measure it, you can't manage it?" How can you add some kind of quantifiable measurement to your goal? If you don't have some way of identifying your progress you'll be asking questions like, "Are we there yet? Are we having fun yet? Is this what success looks like?"

_____

_____

_____

_____

What will it cost?
What will it cost in time, money, resources, and relationships to achieve your goal? It is best to know this going in so that you can plan, save, and apply resources to achieve your North.

_____

_____

_____

_____

What will it cost if I don't?
Most times when people are evaluating a choice they look at the price of something, but they often fail to evaluate what the cost will be if they fail to take action.

_____

_____

_____

_____

What will it cost if you don't make it?

That question to me is always the toughest one, because that's the question that provokes the guilt of regrets. Which would you rather regret, the things that you've done... or the things that you haven't done?

There is an awesome play from the playbook I use to help participants facilitate change in their personal and professional lives. I call it **Life Line.**

A word of caution: A trainer friend called me after using this play in one of his seminars. His opening words to me were, "Do you know they cry during this activity?" I had forgotten to warn him of that little fact, so now I'm warning you.

The reason why the participants cry is explained in the book *Switch: How to Change Things When Change is Hard*, the bestseller by Chip and Dan Heath. In the book, the authors ask the question "Why is it so hard to make lasting changes in our companies, in our communities, in our own lives?"

As it turns out, the primary obstacle is a conflict built into your brain, between two different systems that compete for control: the rational mind and the emotional mind.

The rational mind wants a great beach body; the emotional mind wants that Oreo cookie NOW!!! The rational mind wants to change something at work; the emotional mind loves the comfort of the existing routine. The rational mind wants the house in Hawaii next year; the emotional mind wants a tasty dinner this evening.

The book uses a metaphor to explain the tension between your rational mind and your emotional mind. Visualize a person riding a large elephant. Your rational mind is the Rider, and your emotional mind is the Elephant. The Rider holds the reigns, but control is uncertain because the Rider is so small in relation to the Elephant. If the Elephant and the Rider disagree about which direction to go, the Rider is going to lose.

If you want to change things, you've got to appeal to both the Rider and the Elephant.

Switch provides a three-part framework that can guide you in any situation where you want or need to change behavior. The Heath brothers say in any change situation you need to:

Direct the Rider - What looks like resistance is often a lack of clarity. So provide crystal-clear direction for the Elephant.

Motivate the Elephant - What looks like laziness is often exhaustion. The Rider can only drag the Elephant so far. Eventually the Rider will get tired and give up. So it's critical that you engage people's (and your) emotional side. Encourage the Elephant along the path to change using emotion and not reason.

Shape the Path - What looks like a people problem is often a situational problem, or a problem along the "Path." When you shape the Path, you make change more likely, no matter what's happening with the Rider and the Elephant.

Think of it this way, the Elephant feels comfortable on the Path. The Path is guiding the Elephant who doesn't have to think about where he is going or why. The Elephant likes routine and direction. You simply have to create a Path that heads to the results you're wanting.

When your Elephant goes where your Rider wants, you eliminate conflict, experience real change, and reach your North!

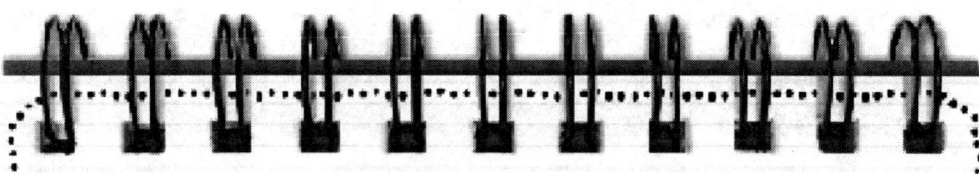

Life Line

|_____|_____|_____|_____|_____|
Date of Birth   **Today's Date**

Think of five major changes you've experienced in your lifetime. Mark an "X" on the timeline when each of the major changes occurred.

Answer these questions for each of the changes:
- What made the change difficult?
- What was the key to your success in dealing with change?
- How did you feel before, during, and after the change?
- How were other things affecting your ability to deal with this change?

It is beneficial for you to share at least one of your changes and answers to these questions with a friend or family member.

Caution: You may get emotional during this activity (The Elephant), and you will also discover when the rational side (The Rider) kicks in that what you have done in the past when dealing with change, whether good or bad, can help you to deal with change in the present and future.

This kind of activity can make change easier because it appeals to both the Elephant and the Rider. This means you will not only find your North, but you will also clear a path for getting there.

Chapter 8
Out of This World Thinking

Sometimes when you're entrenched in the day-to-day, it's hard to innovate or see things from a fresh perspective. But it is at these times that you may need to shake things up by doing some out-of-this-world thinking.

When working with clients, I often hear them use the terms "creative thinking" and "critical thinking" interchangeably even though these phrases are actually different ways of approaching an issue. Each relies on different and specific skills and perspectives. And, both are valuable and distinctly different when developing a powerful strategy.

Creative thinking has three essential characteristics:

> **First, it's productive.** Its primary function is to make something out of nothing.
>
> **Second, it's nonjudgmental.** You cannot generate and judge at the same time.
>
> **Third, it's expansive.** By generating ideas and letting them live by postponing judgment, you tend to get more ideas.

By contrast, critical thinking is analytical, judgmental, and selective. It evaluates actual and possible scenarios using logic and research. When you are thinking critically, you are making choices.

A few years ago, I met a woman in Chicago who is a party-planner. Specifically, she plans princess and pirate parties for "children" of all ages. What a fun idea!

I'm sure you've been to a party that was just . . . well . . . kind of boring. You arrive and don't know anyone, no one makes you feel welcome, the decor consists of a couple of streamers, paper plates, and balloons in matching colors, and the food is only so-so. There is no spirit of fun or camaraderie in the gathering! Something is missing. It's the type of party you wished you'd never gone to, and you start searching for an excuse to get out of there!

Imagine the difference and all the fun your guests would have if you could throw a killer Princess and Pirate theme party. How would it make you feel to throw a party so awesome that your guests have the time of their lives? What would be better than having your guests rave about your party for months and then keep on asking when they can come back for more?

From that lady's description of what she does for her clients, I now pull that idea into many of my breakout sessions. I let the participants loose to innovate and create their own princess and pirate party. I provide tiaras, eye patches, pirate swords, magic wands, etc. I encourage them to let their creativity run wild, not to constrain their ideas with thoughts of potential budgets, liability issues, and whether or not they can actually hire Johnny Depp to appear as a guest celebrity. I tell them to think BIG!

Creative thinking gives you permission to investigate unconventional ideas that will help you differentiate yourself and achieve your vision.

By contrast, critical thinking keeps you on track and helps you develop and evaluate the specific steps you need to create your strategic vision.

By trying simultaneously to think creatively to generate ideas and think critically to judge ideas, you end up sabotaging any chance of success.

Let's take a minute and test your creative thinking. Sometimes this is more difficult then it seems.

Imagine that you have joined Captain Kirk and the crew of the *Starship Enterprise*—"to boldly go where no man has gone before."

You journey to an unexplored universe and join the landing party to visit a newly discovered planet. You hear Captain Kirk say, "Beam us down, Scotty," and suddenly you find yourself in a new world, face-to-face with an alien creature.

Now, take a few minutes, and in the space on the following page, sketch a picture of your alien acquaintance. Be as creative as you can. Don't worry about your drawing skills; just capture the essence of the alien being.

Let me ask you, does the creature have eyes, ears, and a mouth? Does it have a body, arms, and legs?

Despite the instructions to imagine a different universe, and to be creative, you may be surprised at how conventional most of the drawings really are.

There's nothing that prevented you from imagining an energy creature, a vapor or light creature, or even a multi-body or multi-dimension creature. And yet, most people will draw a creature that looks not too unlike people. They repeat the patterns we either see all around us or what people have told us what aliens look like, either through reported sightings or Hollywood movies.

The critical thinking process quickly puts you into a framework of familiarity and patterns. Based on your past experiences, you perceive the world through a frame of reference of 'what you know' and 'what has worked' in the past.

Whether you are trying to solve a problem or create a new opportunity, innovation is simply coming up with an idea and then implementing that idea to add value wherever you are. In your personal life you may be looking for a quicker way to get your work done, or to cut costs. In a business, maybe you are looking for a new way to satisfy customers or develop new revenue streams.

Every time you approach a problem, the natural thing to do is the thing you have always done. You approach the situation by bringing your accumulated knowledge and experience. The more experienced and skilled you are, the more likely you are to assume certain outcomes.

Thinking differently means approaching your daily challenges and habits in new, innovative ways. One of the best ways to think differently is to challenge assumptions.

The difficulty with challenging assumptions is that typically you have already seen that the assumption is true. You ask, "Who can argue with the facts?" In reality, they aren't facts, simply patterns that seem familiar.

Lately, I've been using Michael Michalko's book *Thinkertoys* as a resource in my curriculum design and my workshops. Michalko continually asks his readers to challenge assumptions.

He says, sometimes the way you frame a problem contains an assumption that prevents you from solving it. This frame can stop you from accepting or even looking for innovative ideas.

A technique you can use to challenge a current assumption is to perform what is called a "reverse assumption."

Let's do a reverse assumption together using "vacations" as the example.

First, we'll list some common assumptions we have about vacations. Common assumptions about vacations may be that while on a vacation you:

1. Drive, fly, or take a boat to get to a destination
2. Sleep at a hotel or bed-and-breakfast
3. Go to a restaurant to eat meals

Now, to initiate new ideas and creative thinking, you reverse each assumption, or write down the opposite of each statement:

1. You will not drive, fly, or take a boat to get to destination

2. You will not sleep at a hotel or other traditional lodging

3. You will not eat food at a restaurant

Finally, ask yourself how you would accomplish each reversal.

At first you may be tempted to say, "Impossible," or "It can't be done." But the longer you think about it, you'll soon start creating ideas. You will realize that what you had assumed about vacations does not necessarily have to be true.

Just a few years ago the term "stay-cation" was not a term, yet with the downturn in the economy, unemployment or fear of job loss a reality for so many Americans, the idea of a pricey vacation seemed extravagant and reckless.

Instead of a conventional pricey vacation, like jetting down to Disney World or some exotic locale, a stay-cation might consist of barbecuing at a local state park, visiting a nearby museum, or a visit to a nearby water park. Instead of a hotel, sites like airbnb.com, a community marketplace that connects people who have space to spare with those who are looking for a place to stay, allows you to find unique lodging from an urban apartment to a countryside castle.

Necessity may cause you to challenge your conventional thinking patterns. But what do you think you might discover if you were to examine every day habits and "the way we've always done it" thought patterns with reverse assumptions? How can you free up new ideas in thought provoking ways?

What assumptions do you make about situations in your personal and professional life? If you reversed those assumptions, would you be able to generate new approaches and create solutions to problems you are trying to solve?

As a leader, how often do you think differently? How often do you brainstorm? How often do you hunt for solutions in new environments? Does your organization have a culture that encourages innovation, or is your suggestion box covered in dust?

One of my all time favorite quotes comes from Sam Walton, "The key to success is to get out into the store and listen to what the associates have to say. It's terribly important for everyone to get involved. Our best ideas come from the clerks and stock boys."

You can unleash the innovation in your team, and even your family, when you create a culture where they are rewarded for new ideas.

One idea for the workplace is to host a **Better-Faster-Cheaper Contest**. Ask for ideas on how to speed up processes and save money, while maintaining quality. Maybe offer prizes for the best solutions.

An atmosphere for creative thinking requires holding off judgment on the value of ideas until a later time. If you need innovative ideas, be sure to keep the ideas flowing by separating the creative thinking from the critical thinking process.

You'll find that when you encourage creative thinking, ideas that may have seemed out of this world may indeed launch you to the next level of success and significance.

Reverse Assumptions

What assumptions do you make about situations in your personal and professional life?

_____

_____

_____

If you reversed those assumptions, how would you generate new approaches and create solutions to problems you are trying to solve?

_____

_____

_____

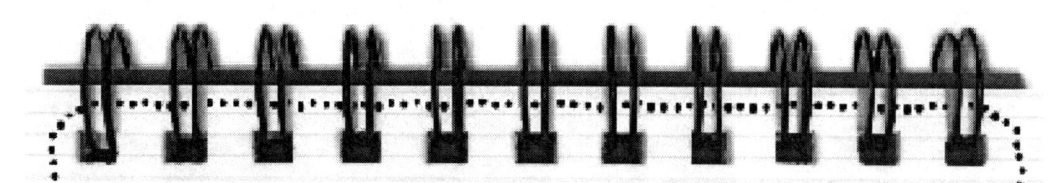

You are not looking for one right answer, but for a way to shake up your conventional thinking patterns so that you can see things from a fresh perspective. This kind of thinking gives you permission to investigate unconventional ideas to help you achieve your vision.

Chapter 9
Where the Ideas Are

How long has it been since your last great idea? To survive, you need to be creative, break through the barriers that are holding you back, and reenergize and refocus your thinking. Free yourself from your own preconceptions, and create an atmosphere that encourages free thinking.

Steve Jobs could have been a failure. He dropped out of college even though his parents struggled to get him into a great school. And, ten years after starting one of the most innovative computer companies in the world, he was fired by the board. Imagine getting fired from a multi-billion dollar company that you started in your own garage.

But what stopped Steve Jobs from being a failure was one simple thing: **Attitude**.

Here's what he told a graduating class at Stanford University in 2005:

> *I didn't see it then, but it turned out that getting fired from Apple was the best thing that could have ever happened to me. The heaviness of being successful was replaced*

by the lightness of being a beginner again, less sure about everything. It freed me to enter one of the most creative periods of my life.

We may not all go on to lead the kind of life that Steve Jobs did after he was fired. But we can duplicate the attitude that he brought when he was fired.

He turned what could have been a humiliating job loss into an incredible period of growth. He turned failure into success.

But you have to be willing to fail. Steve Jobs was renowned for his successes, but he experienced a lot of failures along the way. His eventual success was partly based on his ability to reduce the time and cost associated with failure. In fact, failure became a learning device for him and his company.

> *Creativity doesn't knock. It waits for an invitation.*

You must go where the ideas are. An idea will not find you. When we know where ideas are, and where they are not, you can put yourself in a position to receive a good idea.

What does your creative thinking or workspace feel like? Are you inspired and ready for action, or are you drained from looking at the piles of papers or things to fix, move, or clear up in your workspace? When was the last time you used your dining-room table for a family meal? Last Christmas?

Clutter is the number one enemy of creativity. Even if you believe that you know where everything is in your piles, your brain is using valuable mental processing capability to remember where everything is.

If you want to prepare for creativity, create a space where it can occur.

You also need a sense of tranquility to be creative. Tranquility is an internal state that is free from rush or urgency.

Unfortunately, tranquility is being pushed out of our lives. We have the wrong belief that the busier we are, the more productive and creative we are. However, if we want people to think well under impossible deadlines and inside the orders of 'faster, better, cheaper, more,' we must cultivate internal ease.

For instance, my business partner, who is one of the most creative people I know, has many, many projects on his plate. If he's not traveling around the country giving seminars, he's writing other people's books, editing them, and publishing them. Plus, he teaches online classes for a major university. Any down-time he has, he's pushing after some new activity or experience. It never stops for him.

I have found that if I want him to focus on our business, I need to make sure he has uninterrupted down-time. That is why we schedule weekend masterminds where he disengages as much as possible. That is when his creativity begins to flow.

It actually takes discipline to be tranquil in a creative environment, especially when our society stresses business and adrenaline.

There are some common, negative thinking habits that kill your creativity. Here are a few ways that I have found to kick them to the curb!

Getting Stuck in a Rut – One thing that is guaranteed to kill creativity is doing everything the same way you've always done it. One way to get your brain in gear is to try something totally new. Whether its salsa dancing, pottery, or a medieval reenactment, taking up a new hobby can help shake things up and encourage you to think laterally. For example, you might be inspired to write an article using your new interest as a metaphor for something in your main field of work.

All or nothing thinking - I also call this "black or white" thinking. Everything is all good or all bad... there is nothing in between. You were taught in grade school that there is only 'one right answer' to any question. Haven't you found in life that there are usually many answers that could be 'right' in any given situation? Be open to the possibilities of endless 'right' answers.

Personalization - Do you take things personally? Do you become defensive at the slightest perceived criticism, and think that everything is about you? Try using the **Q-Tip Method** the next time you're tempted to take others ideas and suggestions as a criticism:

>**Quit**
>**Taking**
>**It**
>**Personally**

Tape a Q-tip to your bathroom mirror or computer monitor, if necessary, to remind yourself to quit taking things personally.

Jumping to conclusions - This is when you become a mind reader and a fortune teller. You interpret everything in a negative way without any supporting evidence. You may finish other people's sentences and even tell them what they are thinking. Picture yourself relaxing, back on your heels, and count to five before thinking, responding, or cutting someone else off mid-sentence. Listen to what others have to say—it may be the catalyst to the big idea you are looking for.

Many of us want to be more creative. If you're a blogger, you are searching for a killer idea for your next post. If you work in marketing or advertising, you're trying to come up with that brilliant concept that will bring in a swarm of customers. If you have a creative hobby, like painting or writing, you want the next piece to be a masterpiece.

Sometimes though, have you felt as though you're "just not very creative?" Other people seem to have better ideas and bigger projects. The truth is that there are plenty of ways to help you become more creative—you just have to find the ones that work best for you.

We're often wary of trying new ways of working or new activities because we're afraid we'll fail. But there's no shame in failure—after all, as a baby, you failed countless times at walking, talking, and potty training... but you're an expert in all of those areas now!

If I find 10,000 ways something won't work, I haven't failed. I am not discouraged, because every wrong attempt discarded is another step forward.
—Thomas Edison

Ideas—especially the really great ones that seem to come out of thin air—are the result of your brain working tirelessly and subconsciously to connect past experiences and thoughts and other ideas together in order to form new ideas.

But you cannot, despite how badly you wish it were possible, come up with ideas literally from nothing or out of thin air. Every idea you have is a result of something you've seen or experienced in the past. That's how creativity works.

The more information and ideas and unique experiences you go through, the more your brain has to rely upon when it needs to come up with a new idea down the road.

So, the next time you need a good idea, instead of sitting around and crossing your fingers in hopes that the idea will just "hit you," try a few of the activities I've listed in the next play.

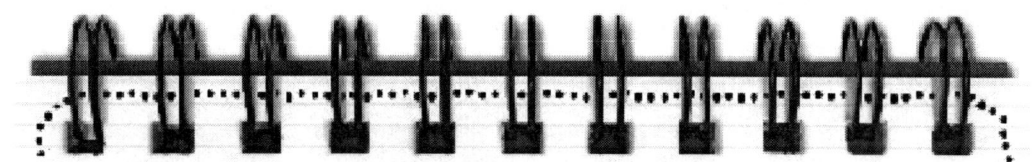

Where the Ideas Are

Read Widely and Deeply - Whatever field you're in, reading can only help. Go to the library and check out some good books, and don't make all of them ones in your area of expertise. Why not get a novel you wouldn't normally read, or a book about a topic you have no knowledge of? This can jump-start your brain into working more creatively as you assimilate new information and mix it with what you already know. What book titles have friends, family, and colleagues recommended? Check the "customers who bought this book also bought..." feature with online retailers.

_____

_____

_____

_____

_____

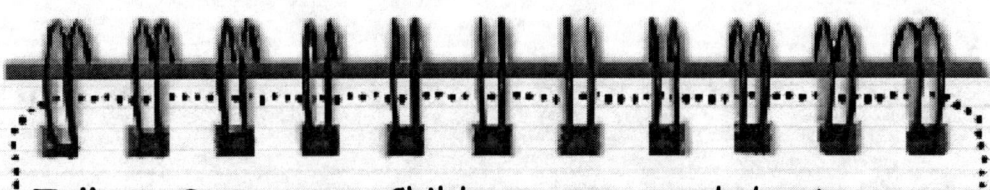

Talk to Strangers - Children are warned about "stranger danger," but as adults, we shouldn't be afraid to talk to new people. We naturally associate with people who are like ourselves (the same income bracket, the same dress sense, the same career or industry). This can stifle our creativity by making us feel that "everyone's just the same." Branch out. Chat with someone you don't know in the cafeteria. Say "hi" to the person next to you in line at the coffee shop. Attend a networking event with professionals who are in a different industry than yours. What strangers will you meet this week?

_____

_____

_____

_____

_____

_____

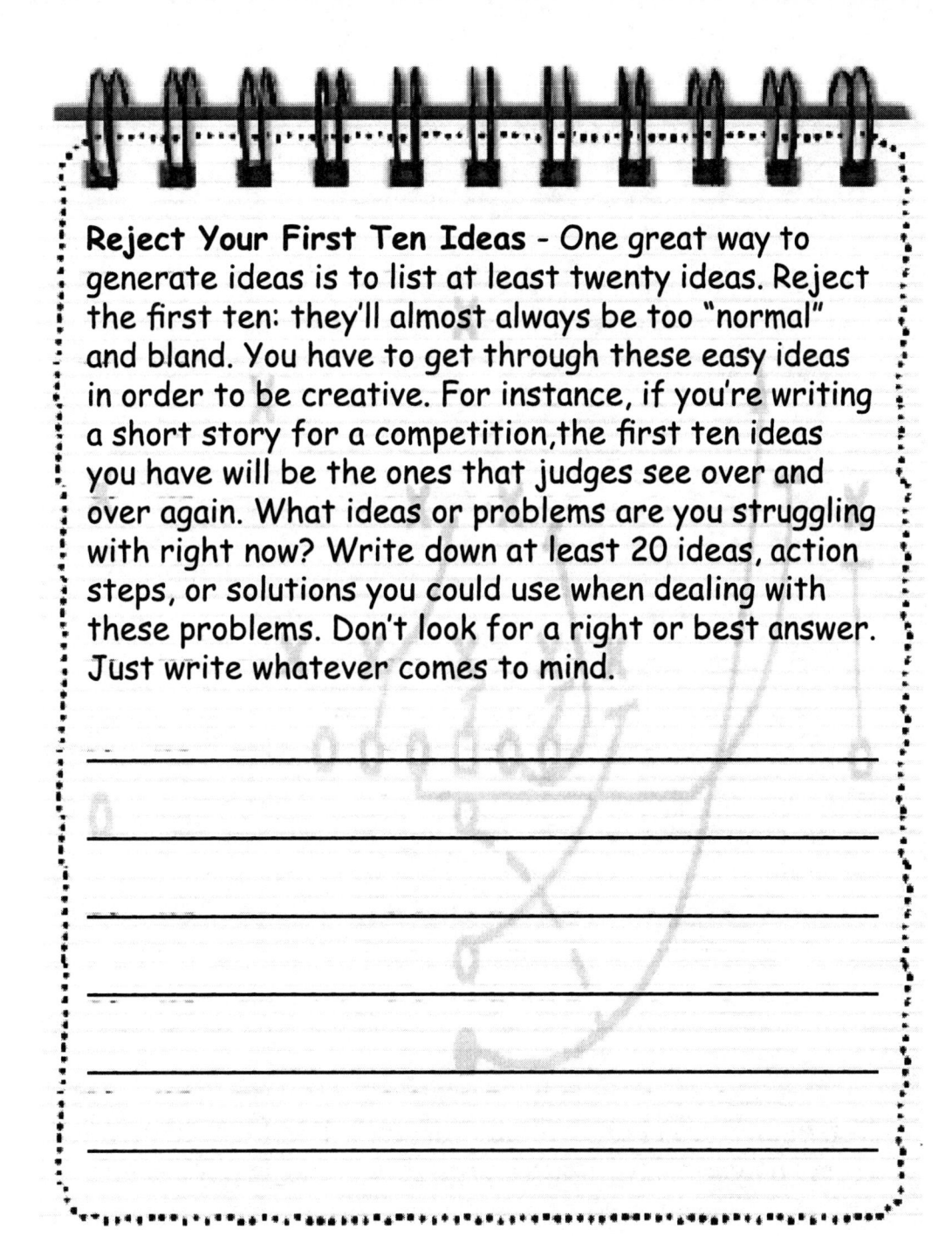

Reject Your First Ten Ideas - One great way to generate ideas is to list at least twenty ideas. Reject the first ten: they'll almost always be too "normal" and bland. You have to get through these easy ideas in order to be creative. For instance, if you're writing a short story for a competition, the first ten ideas you have will be the ones that judges see over and over again. What ideas or problems are you struggling with right now? Write down at least 20 ideas, action steps, or solutions you could use when dealing with these problems. Don't look for a right or best answer. Just write whatever comes to mind.

_____

_____

_____

_____

_____

_____

Remember, you can probably discard the first 10 items on your list... you've probably tried them before.

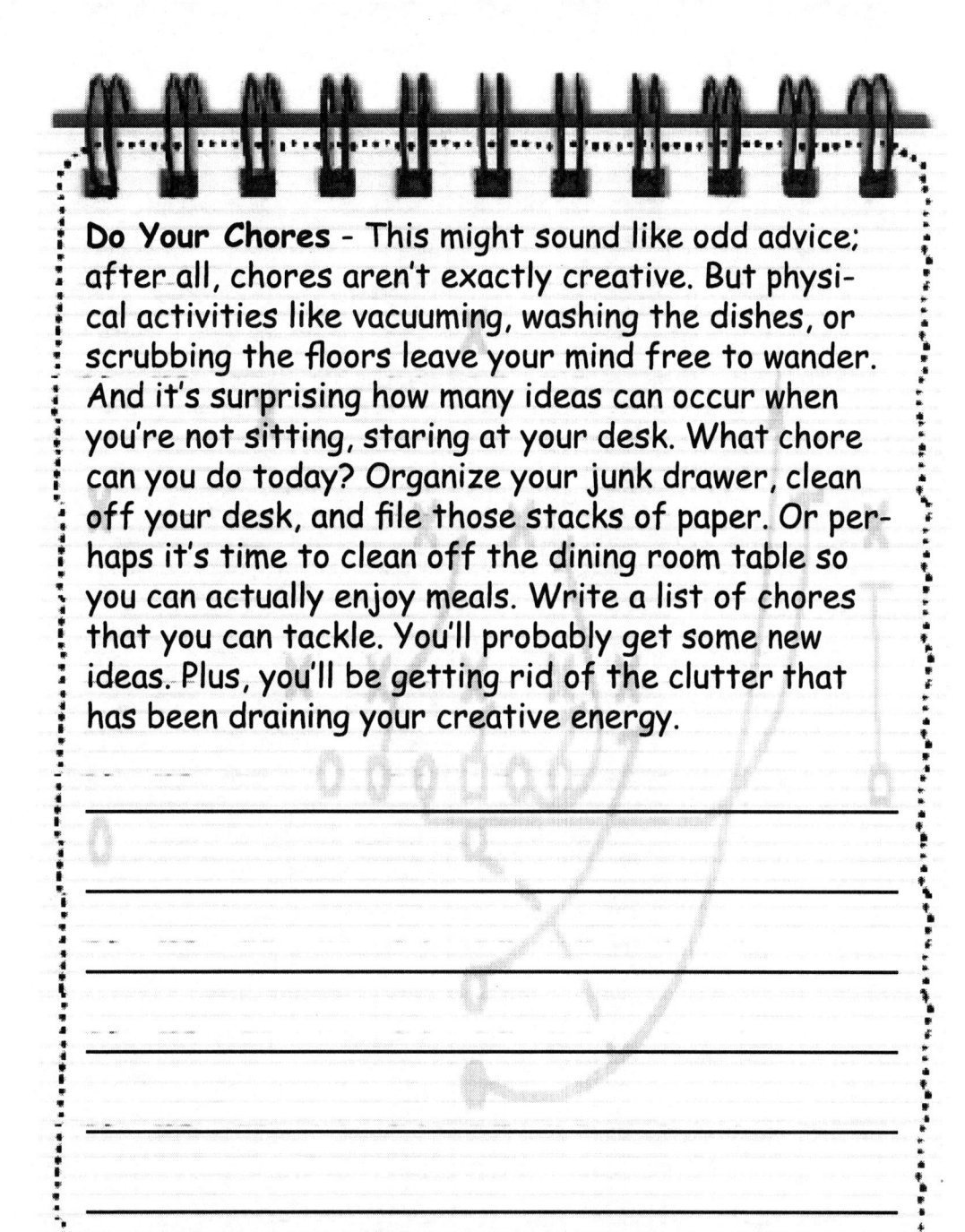

Do Your Chores - This might sound like odd advice; after all, chores aren't exactly creative. But physical activities like vacuuming, washing the dishes, or scrubbing the floors leave your mind free to wander. And it's surprising how many ideas can occur when you're not sitting, staring at your desk. What chore can you do today? Organize your junk drawer, clean off your desk, and file those stacks of paper. Or perhaps it's time to clean off the dining room table so you can actually enjoy meals. Write a list of chores that you can tackle. You'll probably get some new ideas. Plus, you'll be getting rid of the clutter that has been draining your creative energy.

_____

_____

_____

_____

_____

_____

112

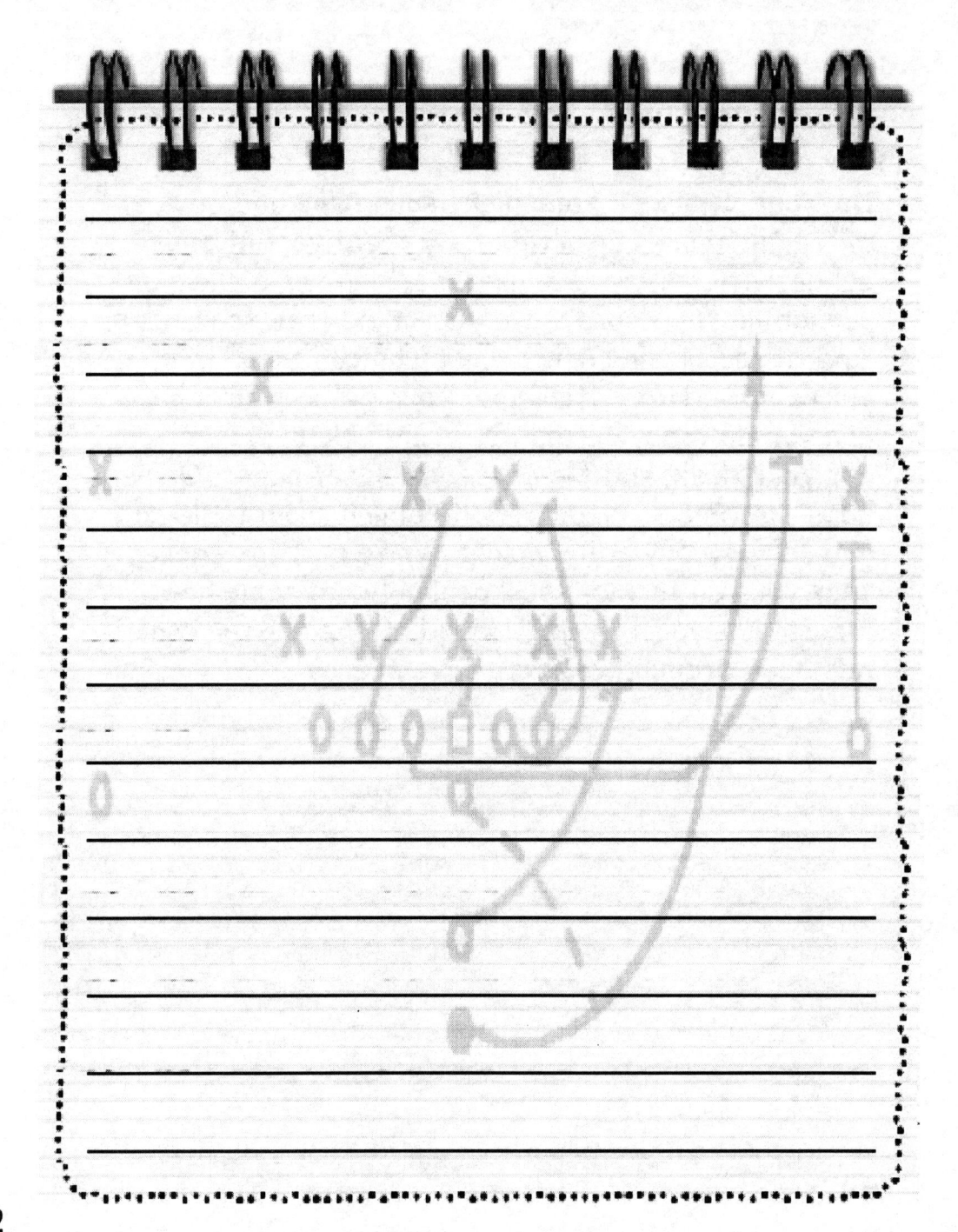

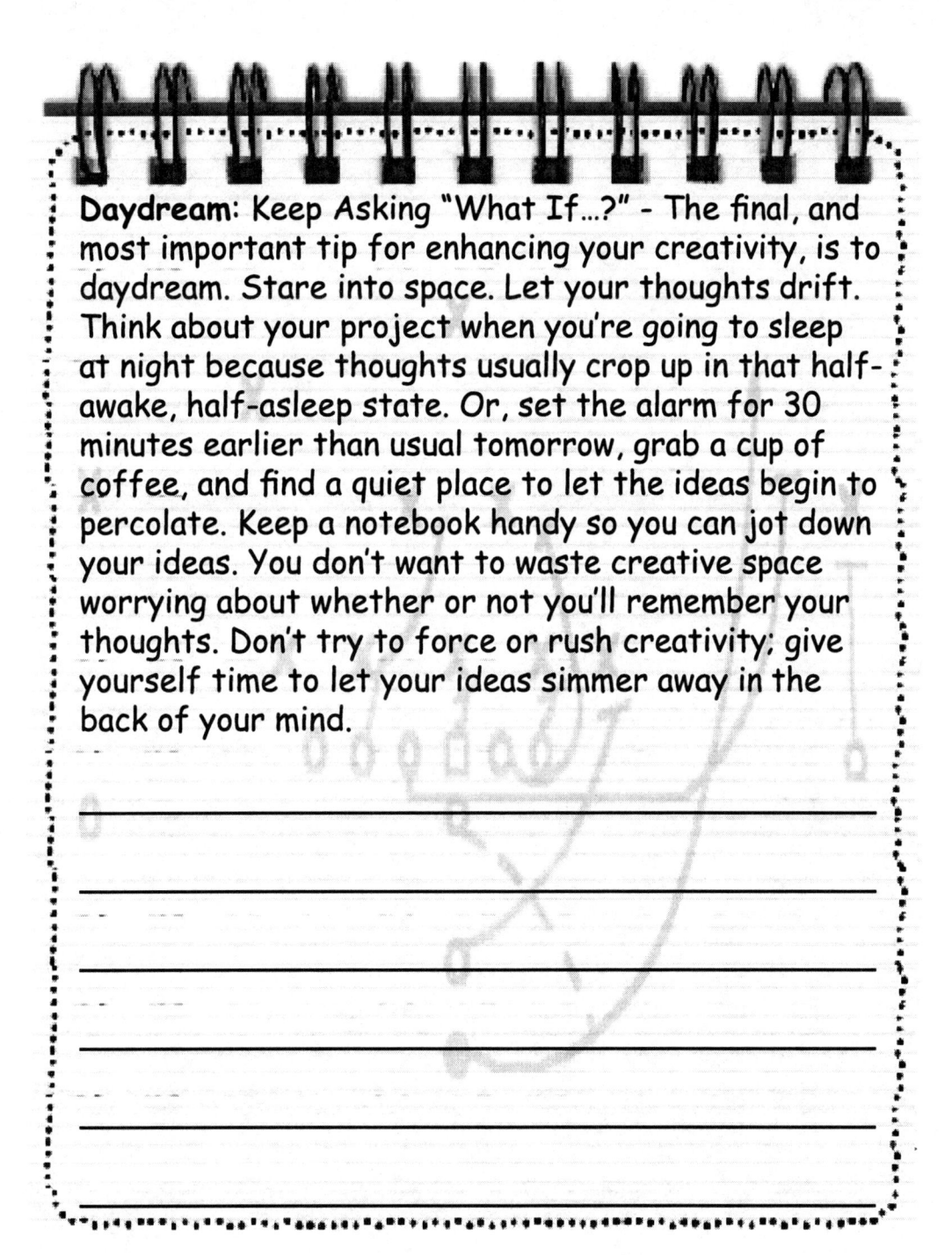

Daydream: Keep Asking "What If...?" - The final, and most important tip for enhancing your creativity, is to daydream. Stare into space. Let your thoughts drift. Think about your project when you're going to sleep at night because thoughts usually crop up in that half-awake, half-asleep state. Or, set the alarm for 30 minutes earlier than usual tomorrow, grab a cup of coffee, and find a quiet place to let the ideas begin to percolate. Keep a notebook handy so you can jot down your ideas. You don't want to waste creative space worrying about whether or not you'll remember your thoughts. Don't try to force or rush creativity; give yourself time to let your ideas simmer away in the back of your mind.

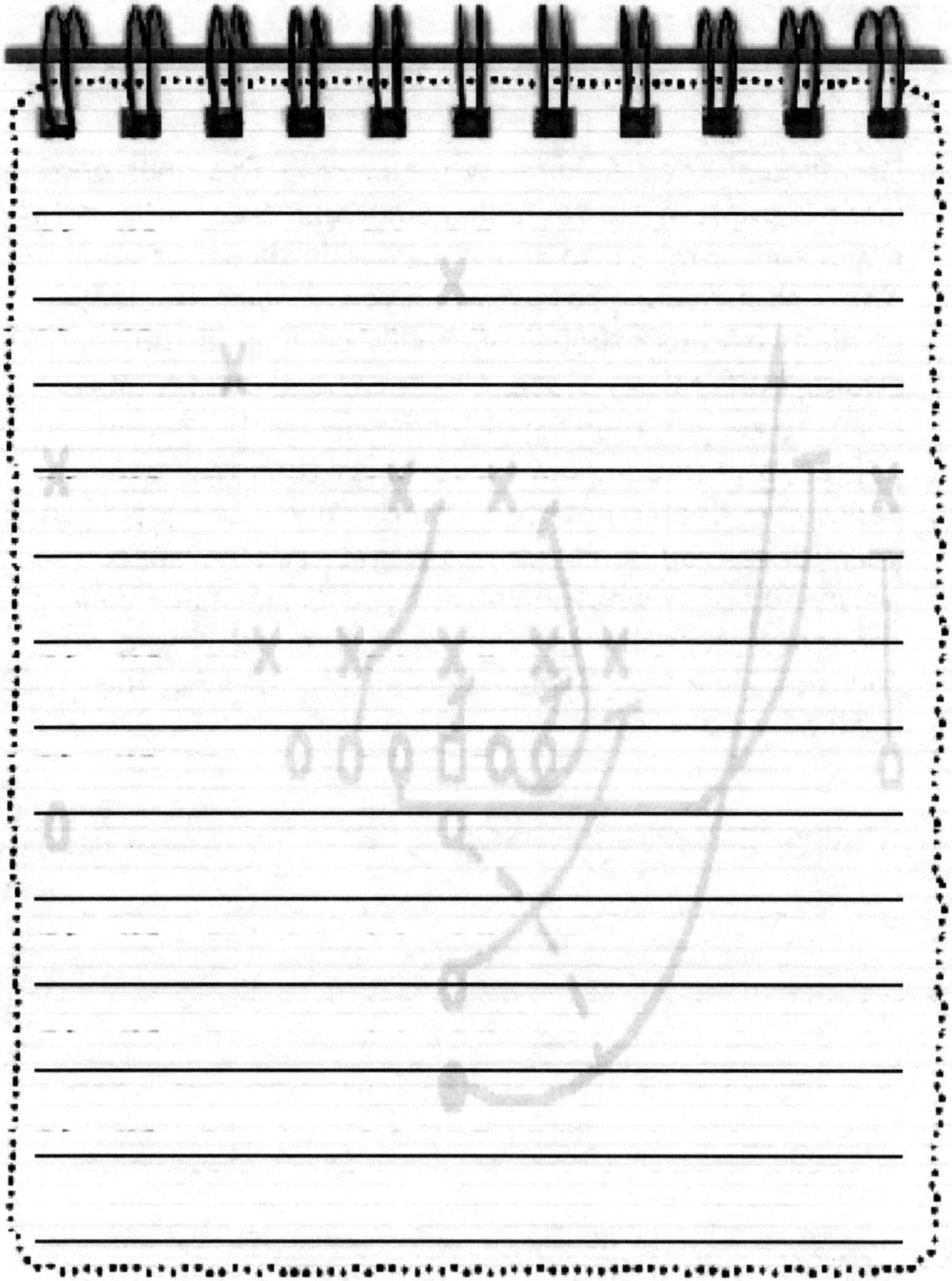

Chapter 10
There, Now, How

We get into a rut when we try to solve every problem with the same solution. The only way to refresh an otherwise repetitive cycle is to identify a problem and really analyze the best way to approach a solution.

Creative thinking takes some effort. And it can cause some discomfort until you get the hang of it. The results, though, are unquestionably awesome.

Each of us started out life creative. As children, when faced with a problem, we always found a way to solve it. We didn't edit ourselves or judge ourselves. And no idea was too silly.

As we aged, though, we became more self-conscious. We fell into "acceptable" ways of doing things. And we were taught in school and in social situations to think a certain way.

Now, when we hear about creativity, most of us see it as the stuff of artists, authors, musicians, and children. We forget how creativity used to come naturally to us. And how creativity helped us solve even the most challenging of situations.

The creative process can be broken down into four distinct processes:

1. Preparation
2. Incubation
3. Illumination
4. Implementation

Preparation: The first phase may seem like work because the process may or may not be fundamentally enjoyable. A musician plays scales, chords, or songs; a writer prepares either by writing, reading, or revising earlier work; an entrepreneur researches problems to solve; a programmer plays with code. In each example, the creative person is going through relatively mundane and tedious processes. But the creative person has learned that this process is necessary to plant the seeds that lead to...

Incubation: In this phase you're percolating. Your conscious and subconscious minds are working on the idea, making new connections, and separating unnecessary ideas. The distractions of everyday life and its immediate concerns can hinder the creative process. However, from this phase comes...

Illumination: Innovative ideas can occur at any time, and "illumination" moments can happen at the most inopportune times, like when you're in the shower, walking the dog, or working out. If you're like me, some of your best ideas "pop" into your head at the most unexpected times. Some have value; some do not.

Old or familiar ideas are fairly easy to remember; new ideas are very difficult to remember unless we record or "capture" them. This is the "Eureka" moment when new ideas hit. Write them down or record them in some way. Whatever is going on in our head, capture it.

Then it's time for...

Implementation: This phase is the one in which the idea you've been preparing and incubating sees the light of day.

It's also when you and others start to evaluate the idea and determine whether it's good or not—but only after they have enough information to see where it's going. This can be frustrating because others don't see the process that went into your idea. Creative ideas don't follow a schedule, and for every good idea, there are at least a few tangents that don't work. But you can't know ahead of time what's going to work and what won't.

It is important that you clearly distinguish between original mistakes made in the course of trying something new and past mistakes repeated out of carelessness. Talk about trying things out, conducting experiments, and learning from what happens. Make learning more important than being "right."

W.L. Gore, known primarily as the maker of Gore-Tex rain gear, encourages employees to develop new ideas through its "dabble time" policy. This policy states that ten percent of a work day can be devoted to personal projects.

In 1995, the company was experimenting with a chemical cousin to Teflon to coat push-pull cables for use in animatronics. Dave Myers, an associate in the company's medical unit, thought the coating might be good for guitar strings and recruited both marketing and manufacturing personnel to work on the project.

Myers' team originally believed that the coating's appeal would be in making strings more comfortable to use. But extensive market research and more than 15,000 guitar-player field tests led the team to realize their real selling point: better sound. The coated strings were only nominally more comfortable than non-coated strings, but they kept their tone longer than conventional guitar strings.

> *Mistakes and failures come in different forms. Don't assume that all mistakes and failures are the same. Like anything else, some are good and some harmful.*

W.L. Gore launched the guitar strings under the brand name ELIXIR Strings, and the company is now the No. 1 seller of acoustic guitar strings.

Creative thinking is a skill like any other. It can be taught, it can be developed, and it can be nurtured.

It's true, anyone can be taught to think better, to understand more clearly, think more creatively, and plan more effectively. The creative process begins with work and ends with work.

But thinking creatively isn't enough. Once you pick a solution, you must put it into action.

Years ago, when my friends and I were just starting our careers, one of the couples leveraged like crazy to buy an old

Victorian home. It was a real stretch to save money for the down payment.

I remember the day I helped them move in. I was in the kitchen unpacking boxes of china and crystal when the realtor came in and said to my friend, "This is a fixer upper, a real fixer upper. Now, you've got to make sure that you make a list of all the things that you want to get fixed and get it done within the first six months."

My friend replied, "Are you for real? This old house? With the down payment, closing costs, taxes, and so on, we don't have much left. Besides, we're disciplined people. Over the next few years we'll be able to do what we want to do."

The realtor said, "After six months, you get used to it. It seems to fit. You get used to stepping over the creaky stair, and won't even see the cracking linoleum here in the kitchen."

And you know what? The realtor was right! When my friends were relocating to a new city five years later, they put the house on the market. The things they hadn't fixed in the first six months, still weren't fixed.

Things like this can happen to you. You start to roll forward a bit, and then get satisfied, and stop. Everyday busyness and inertia overcome you. At the first sign of any success you pause to celebrate. But all you've done is put on a fresh coat of paint and straightened the shutters.

How can you set goals that will keep the transition moving forward?

Ideally, your goals should be as specific as possible. The more specific a goal is, the more likely everyone involved will have a common, shared understanding about what it means. That's important.

But most important, do it now. Don't wait. When you wait, you will be comfortable with the new normal.

Creativity means little without application. Once you have the idea, take action.

And that's where you'll discover the rewards of thinking differently.

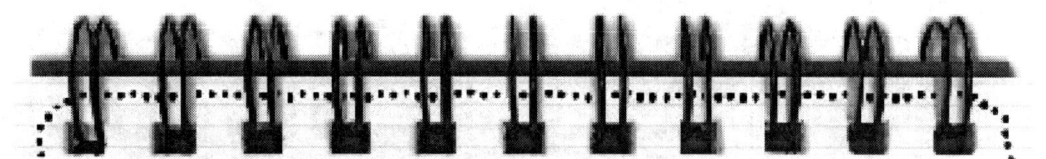

There, Now, How

Let's create a roadmap for change, it's called the **There, Now, How** play. Here's how it works: Go back to the Matrix that you created in Chapter 1. Pick one of the items you identified as very important to your success, but that you are not doing anything about right now.

Since a picture is worth a thousand words, draw it out on the chart on the next page.

Capture on the left side of the chart where you are now, scattering the words and adding images to that area. Describe what the current state of the business, career, finances, health, or any particular process is right now.

Then go to the right side and imagine "There," and imagine the best case scenario for one year from today. What are you or your family members saying? What are sales like? What is the work environment? Where are you in health and fitness, debt reduction, retirement savings, etc.?

124

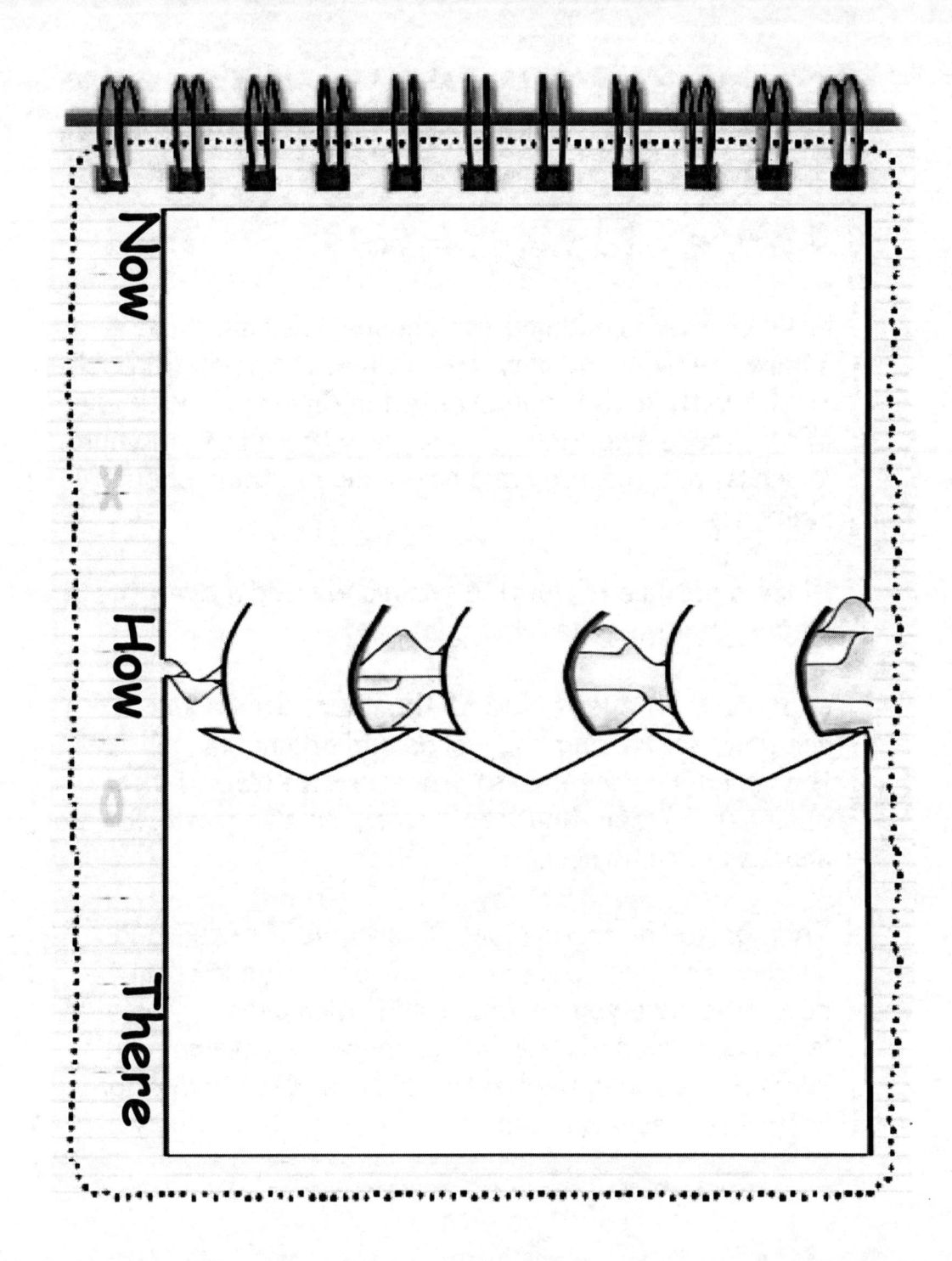

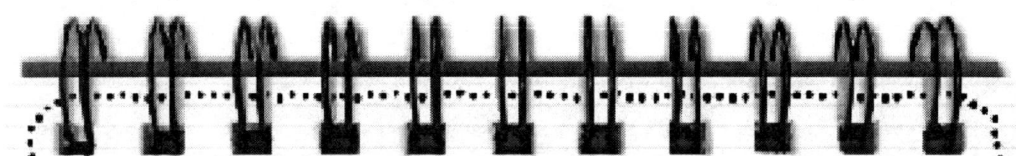

Now, look at the gap between the two, and come up with the three bold steps you believe you need to take to get you from **Now** to **There**. Look at both sides. Close your eyes for a second. This allows the brain to restructure what it sees and mash up what you see with what you know or have read about or even dreamed.

Then think of the boldest things you can do to get there. Choose the top three, and write them on the three arrows in the center of the picture.

Make copies of the blank chart, enlarge it, blow it up to poster size, and hang it on your dining room or office wall.

Do the **There, Now, How** play for each of the items that you identified in Chapter 1 as very important for your future and your success that you are not doing now.

Prologue
...To Thinking Differently NOW!!

Instead of wondering, "What were you thinking?" now you have your roadmap for change.

Henry Ford once said, "Thinking is the hardest work there is, which is the probable reason why so few engage in it."

Today, the only significant differentiator for you, your career, and your success in relationships, health, finances, or spirituality is how well you can use all the information available to you. Your success and happiness will be based on how effectively you sift through all the information available to you, evaluate it, transform it into new ideas, and maximize its economic potential.

Change is inevitable... growth is optional.

You cannot stay the same as you are today. You're either getting better or you're getting worse. When you become complacent, you enter into mediocrity. And mediocrity leads to irrelevancy.

It's easy to accept mediocrity because you can find a lot of people to surround yourself with who are mediocre. It's easy to think, "I'm OK with the way things are" when you're surrounded with complacent people.

But those people are not going where you're going. And complacency will not get you to where you want to go. You need different results, which means you need to break away from conventional thinking.

Your ability to think better—and differently—will soon become the most significant competitive advantage you can claim. Thinking better is what it is all about.

Be creative and find the one, two, or three things that you can do differently to create the change you need.

And then celebrate your success!!!!

About the Author

Featured on the cover of *Bloomberg Businessweek*, Monica Cornetti has been designated as "one of the best" entrepreneurial training experts. She works with individuals and organizations who want to learn how to think differently to achieve different results.

Monica is a highly sought-after speaker because of her spunkiness and emphasis on fun while learning. She is the author of the acclaimed book, *Your Face Isn't Finished Until Your Lipstick Is On: Rules of the Women's Success Game.*

Monica's client list includes: The Association of Small Business Development Centers, Texas Tech, Shell Oil, Infinisource, Proctor & Gamble, The Nature Conservancy, American Fidelity, FM Global, American Society of Women Accountants, The Society for Human Resource Management, Las Vegas Chamber of Commerce, MEED Center, International Association of Administrative Professionals, HR Southwest, City of Price, Utah, Greater El Paso Credit Union, and Severn Savings Bank.

Monica is a graduate of Seton Hill with a BA in psychology, and The University of Houston-Victoria where she earned a Masters Degree in Economic Development and Entrepreneurship, chosen by Forbes Small Business as one of the top online programs for Entrepreneurship in the nation.

Her audiences from Guam to Georgia and Maui to Maine give her Perfect 10 reviews!

Contact Information:
MonicaCornetti.com
monica@MonicaCornetti.com

Hire Monica to Speak

Do you feel that your organization is capable of higher productivity?

Are you looking for a tangible way to boost staff morale?

Is it time to get more from your customer engagement or training and development programs?

When it comes to choosing a dynamic, motivational speaker for your next event, you'll find no one more qualified or gifted than Monica Cornetti.

Monica is a highly sought after international keynote speaker and trainer. She is considered one of the leading authorities on entrepreneurial thinking and leadership in the business. Her emphasis is always on fun as she delivers high-energy, high-content sessions, along with a plan for application in the real world.

With over 150 national, regional, and local speaking engagements each year, her keynotes are guaranteed to make you laugh ... make you cry ... and in the end provide your audience with information and motivation to create real change in their personal and professional lives!

If you are looking for an unforgettable speaker who will leave your audience wanting more, then book Monica Cornetti today.

Please email monica@monicacornetti.com, or call (972-951-3314) and Monica or one of her booking agents will get in touch with you to book your event and schedule a pre-speech interview.

Go to www.monicacornetti.com for demo videos and a complete list of topics.